BOTANY FOR NATURALISTS

A Colour Guide

John Presland

ISBN: 1492315346
ISBN-13: 9781492315346

ACKNOWLEDGEMENTS

This book owes much to the very many people who have contributed over the years to the knowledge which has enabled me to write it. It would be impossible to name them all, but they have my grateful thanks. Many thanks to John Roberts and John Kerr for providing photos of theirs which I could not find in my own collection. I would also like to thank my wife Pat for her tolerance of my many hours of writing and for acting as a sounding board.

INTRODUCTION

This is an illustrated account of botany for amateur naturalists, aiming to provide the information they need to pursue an interest in the subject in the most enjoyable and interesting way. As much of it as possible is presented pictorially, almost all photographically, with pictures in each plate accompanied by explanatory text.

Botany is a biological science. Science uses careful, objective observation to establish facts, and seeks to explain and organise them to give better understanding of them and to make predictions of future events. This book is based on the findings of such activity.

Botanists study plants, rather than other growing things. But what is a plant? Traditionally, it included any living thing which was green and manufactured its food from carbon dioxide, water and mineral salts taken in from the surrounding air, soil or water. This was seen as a major distinction from animals, which did not make their own food, but obtained it ready-made by eating plants or other animals. Further, most living things called plants did not obviously move from place to place by their own efforts, whereas most animals did. Fungi do not manufacture their own food, but were called plants because of their appearance.

Nowadays, the picture is more complex. Algae, fungi and lichens, once treated as plants by botanists, are now regarded as belonging to kingdoms separate from those of plants and animals. However, as Evert and Eichhorn, authors of the latest edition of the very comprehensive and up-to-date *Raven Biology of Plants*, say, "they are normally considered part of the botanical portion of the curriculum", so they are included. Though native British plants are the main focus here, plants from elsewhere, including some cultivated in gardens, are occasionally used to illustrate points of particular interest. Further, botany cannot be studied without taking some account of the animals which live and interact with them, so they also have a small place in the book.

The account here aims to be as thorough as possible without requiring specialised resources. For the most part, it does not depend on looking through a microscope, nor using any other equipment or materials rarely found outside scientific contexts. It covers: the structure of flowering plants; the way flowering plants grow, behave, reproduce and adapt to their environments; naming, classifying and identifying plants; conifers; ferns and their allies; mosses and liverworts; algae, fungi and lichens; communities of living things; recording; conservation and biodiversity; and a glance at inheritance and evolution

Diagrams are the author's own. All photographs are believed to be his unless otherwise stated. English names are spelt in what the author considers the most helpful and easily remembered way.

LIST OF PLATES

PLATE 1: FLOWERING PLANT STRUCTURE

Every plant is different from every other plant, even if in small ways. The diagram of a hypothetical typical flowering plant is a model to use as a starting point for looking at and understanding the many variations which occur in different plants. It consists of a root, a stem, leaves borne on the stem and flowers grouped into inflorescences. The flowers develop into fruits, so these are implicitly included. The angle between a leaf and the stem is called the leaf axil. In the axil of each leaf is a tight bunch of overlapping leaves called an axillary bud. Some of these axillary buds grow into lateral stems (branches). At the base of each leaf there may be additional, often leaf-like, structures called stipules. There is usually a terminal bud, which is a leaf bud in the early stages but often a flower bud later. Between the leaves and the inflorescence, and often extending up into the latter, leaf-like structures called bracts commonly occur.

Though the model is applicable to most plants, it is occasionally difficult to apply directly. There are plants that do not have roots, but just rest on a surface or blow around in the wind. Some plants, such as Coltsfoot (*Tussilago farfara*) have their flowers and their main leaves visible at completely different times, so that it is not obvious that they belong to each other. Butcher's Broom (*Ruscus aculeatus*) does not have recognizable leaves, but has flattened leaf-like stems called cladodes which have tiny remnants of leaves on them and on which the flowers are borne. Stemless/Dwarf Thistle (*Cirsium acaule*) typically does not have noticeable stems, both leaves and flowers being more or less at ground level. Duckweeds (*Lemna* species) have no leaves, consisting of flattened leaf-like stems which float on the water surface with roots descending and minute flowers on top with no stalks.

This and the following plates focus on what can be illustrated pictorially. Some plants species are distinguishable in other ways. *Allium* species such as Ramsons or Wild Garlic (*Allium ursinum*) have a distinctive onion or garlic smell. Plants in the Deadnettle family (*Lamiaceae*), such as mints, often have a herby smell and taste. Many plants in the Cress family (*Brassicaceae*) contain substances called isothiocyanates, which give a bite to their flavour which appeals to some and puts off others.

Only the most frequently used or particularly helpful terms are included. If others are encountered, *The Cambridge Illustrated Glossary of Botanical Terms* by Hickey and King (2000) or the glossary of a comprehensive flora should be consulted. The third edition of Stace's *New Flora of the British Isles* (2011) is the standard one used today.

In the pages that follow, the main parts of the typical plant are covered in order - stem, root, leaf, inflorescence, flower and fruit. The photos are examples and do not imply that the featured species is always as shown.

Structure of a typical flowering plant

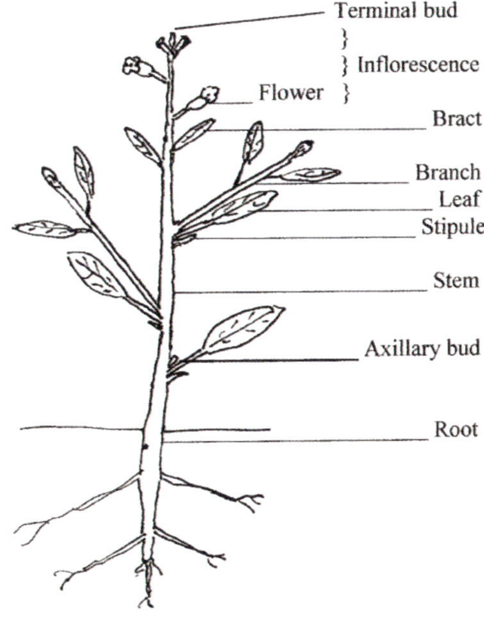

Coltsfoot - flowers but no leaves

Butcher's Broom - cladode bearing flower

Coltsfoot - leaves but no flowers

Stemless/Dwarf Thistle - no stem

Duckweed - flat, floating stem

PLATE 2: THE VARIETY OF STEMS

The stem in our model plant is thin in relation to its length, upright, straight, and cylindrical and bears leaves and flowers. In a particular species, however, it can be thick and woody, as in trees and shrubs, or relatively narrow and soft, as in herbaceous plants, though some of the latter can develop some wood as they mature. The margins are covered by a protective layer, which is thick and corky and called bark in trees and shrubs, but typically thinner and referred to as the epidermis in herbaceous plants. The inner part is either solid or hollow.

Stems may be branched or unbranched. The most common forms of branching are opposite and alternate. Alternate includes both first on one side and then on the other, as in Hawthorn (*Crataegus monogyna*), and in a spiral up and round the stem, as in Broad-leaved Dock (*Rumex obtusifolius*). Sometimes, however, the stem just forks into two. More than two branches can come off the stem at the same point. Where the branches are in opposite pairs, it is commonly the case that each pair is at right angles to the ones immediately above and below, an arrangement called decussate, as in Dogwood (*Cornus sanguinea*).

Typically, the stem is erect and self-supporting. In plants that are biennial or perennial (living for two or more than two years respectively), they are typically larger and, needing more support because of this, often become woody. Other plants have no stems, or weak stems which cannot support themselves in an erect position and are more or less prostrate, as in Creeping Jenny (*Lysimachia nummularia*). Stems can differ in cross-section. Most are round, as in Hogweed (*Heracleum sphondylium*) but some are triangular and some square, as in White Deadnettle (*Lamium album*). There may also be longitudinal ridges. The stems of many plants have small structures on their surface. Some have flattened wings down the sides. Others have thorns or stings. Stems can be hairy or not, and the hairs can be simple or forked and lie flat against the stem or project, and can be distributed in a wide variety of ways. Others have glands, which are commonly spherical objects and are sometimes on the ends of hairs, as in American Willowherb (*Epilobium ciliatum*). These glands normally secrete substances, so the part of the plant they inhabit is often sticky.

Stems also vary in colour. Most herbaceous plant stems are green because they contain the green substance chlorophyll which is essential for producing foodstuffs. Plants which obtain their foodstuffs ready-made, such as parasites from a host plant on which they grow and saprophytes which get it from decaying remains of living things in the soil, are not normally green. Plant stems can also have other colours - the green colour can be blue-tinged (glaucous), or stems often go red or purple in part, as in Hemlock (*Conium maculatum*), or wholly. Damage to a stem sometimes reveals coloured sap - white, yellow or orange, for instance. In Yellow-juiced poppy (*Papaver lecocqui*) it is yellow.

More specialised stem structures are shown in Plates 23 and 24.

Hawthorn - alternate

Broad-leaved Dock - spiral

Dogwood - opposite, decussate

Creeping Jenny - prostrate

Hogweed - hollow, circular, ridged, hairy

White Deadnettle - square, hairy, hollow

American Willowherb - glandular hairs

Hemlock - purple blotches, ridged

Yellow-juiced Poppy - yellow sap

PLATE 3: THE VARIETY OF ROOTS

Roots are normally cylindrical and protected on the outside by a firm covering called the exodermis and sometimes by a corky layer. Small hairs (root hairs) project from the surface. Roots can be single or branched and deep or spread out in shallow soils, as in Beech trees growing on chalk.

There are two main forms of root. One is the tap root, a single root which may branch, as in Cow Parsley (*Anthriscus sylvestris*). The other is the adventitious root, a number of which commonly form at the junction with the main stem, as in Ivy-leaved Speedwell (*Veronica hederifolia*). They are also found along prostrate or underground stems, and on corms and bulbs. Roots can also develop as storage organs or other structures shown in Plates 23, 26 and 42.

Cow Parsley - taproot

Ivy-leaved Speedwell - adventitious roots

PLATE 4: ARRANGEMENTS OF LEAVES

Leaves vary even on the same plant and can show a continuous range of forms between species. Botanical terms are used to describe these, but sometimes a plant can be in between two of them or show both. The captions simply describe what is present in the photos, which may not always be typical of the species.

Leaves vary in their arrangement on the stem. They can all be at the base, or arranged in the various ways described earlier for branches, since branches normally occur in leaf axils. So they can be opposite, decussate, alternate (one on one side then one on the next), spiral, in whorls, or there can be just one leaf, or a pair. Some plants have none at all and sometimes there are only tiny scale leaves. Sometimes there is a single pair or whorl of leaves at one point. Leaves are occasionally in joined pairs which encircle the stem, referred to as perfoliate. The examples used are Daisy (*Bellis perennis*), Wall Cotoneaster (*Cotoneaster horizontalis*), Petty Spurge (*Euphorbia peplus*), Purple Loosestrife (*Lythrum salicaria*), Herb Paris (*Paris quadrifolia*), Teasel (*Dipsacus fullonum*), Cleavers (*Galium aparine*) and Catsear (*Hypochaeris radicata*).

Daisy - all at the base

Wall Cotoneaster - alternate

Petty Spurge - spirally arranged

Purple Loosestrife - opposite and decussate

Herb Paris - one whorl

Teasel - pairs joined at base

Cleavers - whorl with many leaves

Catsear - scale leaves

PLATE 5: OVERALL FORMS OF LEAVES

Leaves vary in their overall form. Most have a flat part called the lamina and a leaf stalk called the petiole, but the petiole is often absent and in a few cases the lamina. A leaf without a petiole is called sessile. Sometimes sessile leaves clasp the stem (amplexicaul), sometimes with projections beyond it called auricles. The base of a leaf can also form a sheath round the stem - or go down it with narrow leaf-like “wings”, when the leaf is said to be decurrent.

The overall form can also be simple (single and undivided, sometimes incompletely divided), or compound (completely divided into parts). The parts of a compound leaf are called leaflets and the parts of an incompletely divided leaf are called lobes. Leaflets or lobes can be in two rows, one on each side of the central axis and in opposite pairs. If these divisions are complete, the leaf is called pinnate. If only partial, it’s pinnatifid. If it’s almost to the centre, it’s pinnatisect. Where a terminal leaflet is also present, the leaf is called imparipinnate, whereas if there isn’t it’s called paripinnate. Where the terminal division of an imparipinnate leaf is large and the others progressively smaller, it is called lyrate and if, additionally, the others are directed downwards it called runcinate. Sometimes the leaflets or lobes are divided again, when they are called bipinnate, and further divisions labeled as tri- , quadri- etc also occur.

Leaves can also be divided so that all the leaflets or lobes radiate from a common central point and this arrangement is called palmate. Where there are two such leaflets, the leaf is bifoliate, and you can also have trifoliate (or ternate), quadrifoliate, etc. There are also palmatisect and palmatifid patterns. Leaflets or lobes of a palmate leaf can be divided again.

These forms are illustrated by photos of Chicory (*Cichorium intybus*), Common Comfrey (*Symphytum officinale*), Giant Fescue (*Schedonurus giganteus*), Common St John’s Wort (*Hypericum perforatum*), Dog’s Mercury (*Mercurialis perennis*), Ash (*Fraxinus excelsior*), Bush Vetch (*Vicia sepium*), Nipplewort (*Lapsana communis*), Dandelion (*Taraxacum officinale*), Hemlock (*Conium maculatum*) and Horse Chestnut (*Aesculus hippocastanum*).

Chicory - sessile, clasping with auricles, pinnatifid

Common Comfrey - decurrent , winged

Giant Fescue - sheathing

Common St John's Wort - sessile, simple, entire

Dog's Mercury - petiolate, simple, entire

Ash - imparipinnate

Bush Vetch - paripinnate

Nipplewort - pinnati-sect-pinnate, lyrate

Hemlock - bi- to tri-pinnate, petiolate,

Dandelion - runcinate

Horse Chestnut - palmate

PLATE 6: LEAF AND LEAFLET SHAPES

Any leaf or leaf part can be of one of a variety of overall shapes - the most common being linear (narrow with parallel sides), filiform (threadlike), lanceolate (narrowing gradually at top and bottom but broadest in the lower half and much longer than broad), oblanceolate (like lanceolate but broadest above the middle), ovate (narrowing at top and bottom but broadest in lower half and not much longer than broad), obovate (like ovate but broadest above the middle), elliptic (narrowing at top and bottom but broadest in the middle), oblong (longer than broad, parallel-sided but narrowing abruptly at top and bottom), orbicular (circular), reniform (kidney-shaped) and rhombic (diamond-shaped). Deltate (triangular) and spathulate (paddle-shaped) feature regularly in flora glossaries, though it is hard to find unambiguous examples. The apex can be acute (pointed), obtuse (blunt), aristate (with a stiff bristle projecting at the top), acuminate (tapering to a short drawn-out tip), mucronate (with a short narrow point), cuspidate (narrowing fairly abruptly to a short drawn out tip), apiculate (narrowing abruptly to a small point), or emarginate (notched at the apex). At the base it can be rounded, cordate (heart-shaped), cuneate (broadening in straight lines from the base, like an inverted triangle), truncate (straight and more or less at right angles to the petiole when there is one), hastate (flat and drawn out into a point at each side) or sagittate (like the point of an arrow). The margins can be entire or indented, and then serrate (finely toothed like a saw), doubly serrate (the serrations themselves serrate), dentate (more broadly toothed) or crenate (rounded between indentations), crisped (curled), sinuate (with a side-to-side wavy outline) or undulate (with an up and down wavy outline). Peltate leaves have the petiole attached centrally on the underside of a flat lamina. Crow Garlic (*Allium vineale*) has stems which appear linear but are actually hollow tubes. In many cases, the leaf form can be intermediate between two or more options, in which case identification books usually say something like “ovate-lanceolate”, or range from one to the other, described as, for instance, “ovate to lanceolate”.

In Plate 4, Purple Loosestrife shows leaves which are lanceolate, Petty Spurge elliptical, Daisy spathulate, Cleavers aristate and Wall Cotoneaster mucronate. In Plate 5, oblanceolate leaflets are shown in Horse Chestnut, rhombic and cuneate leaves in Dog’s Mercury, leaf rounded at the base and with entire margins in Common St John’s Wort, leaves acute in Ash and notched leaflets in Bush Vetch. Other forms are shown here in Common Star of Bethlehem, (*Ornithogalum umbellatum*), Black Medick (*Medicago lupulina*), Silver Birch (*Betula pendula*), Fennel (*Foeniculum vulgare*), Lungwort (*Pulmonaria officinalis*), Large-leaved Lime (*Tilia platyphyllos*), Winter Heliotrope (*Petasites fragrans*), Common Sorrel (*Rumex acetosa*), Wall Pennywort (*Umbilicus rupestris*), Spear-leaved Orache (*Atriplex prostrata*) and cultivated cabbage (*Brassica oleracea* cultivar). Less common ones can be found in the publications cited in Plate 1.

Common Star of Bethlehem - linear

Black Medick - obovate, apiculate

Silver Birch - triangular, doubly serrate

Fennel - segments filiform

Lungwort - ovate, cordate, acuminate

Large-leaved Lime - ovate, cuspidate, serrate

Winter Heliotrope - crenate, rounded, reniform

Common Sorrel - obtuse, sagittate

Wall Pennywort - peltate, orbicular, crenate

Spear-leaved Orache - deltate, truncate, hastate

Horseradish - undulate

Cultivated cabbage - young leaf sinuate

PLATE 7: LEAF SURFACES AND SPECIAL FEATURES

There are considerable variations in the leaf surface. Sometimes it is hairy, sometimes not (glabrous). Sometimes it is covered by a woolly or velvety (tomentose) mass of hairs, or there can be white silky hairs covering the undersides. Hairs can be branched in various ways. The surface can have a wrinkled appearance (rugose) or have blisters at the base of hairs. There can also be colour variations, such as a whitish stripe down the middle or mottling or a bluish cast (glaucous). Common St John's Wort has transparent and black, dot-like oil glands. The surface can also be prickly or spiny. Sometimes veins can be seen, sometimes a single one in the centre, sometimes a number of parallel main veins or with various patterns of branching.

Leaves and leaf-like structures can be different on different parts of the stem. They can be small and often colourless on underground parts or sometimes on stems, when they are called scale leaves. Leaves in the inflorescence are usually called bracts and are normally differently shaped from the others. The first leaves which emerge from a seed are often different from later leaves and are called cotyledons. Many plants have additional leaf-like structures called stipules where a leaf joins the stem, sometimes joining to provide it with a protective sheath. Grasses have a leaf-like structure called a ligule where the leaf sheath joins the blade, often difficult to see and photograph. Another difference is between leaves that fall in the winter (deciduous) and those that remain on the tree (persistent, the plant being called evergreen).

There is a whole range of less typical forms of leaves, which can be seen as adaptations to particular environments. Some, for instance, are thick and fleshy, and some bear tendrils for climbing. Some leaves have no lamina, but a flattened petiole known as a phyllode. Some water plants have underwater leaves of one shape and aerial or floating leaves of different shapes. These are shown in Plates 5, 23, 24, 26, 27, 42, 46 and 47.

Plate 4 shows prickly leaves with a single prominent vein in Cleavers. Plate 5 shows glabrous leaves, transparent and black glands and three main veins with minimal branching in Common St John's Wort. Plate 6 shows white mottling in Lungwort, and fleshy leaves in Wall Pennywort. Other characters are shown here in Field Forget-me-not (*Myosotis arvensis*), Snow in Summer (*Cerastium tomentosum*), Great Mullein (*Verbascum thapsus*), Bristly Oxtongue (*Helminthotheca echioides*), Ivy (*Hedera helix*), Yellow-wort (*Blackstonia perfoliata*), Wood Sage (*Teucrium scorodonia*), Hoary Plantain (*Plantago media*), Astrantia (*Astrantia major*) and Red Clover (*Trifolium pratense*).

Field Forget-me-not - hairy

Snow in Summer - tomentose

Great Mullein - woolly

Bristly Oxtongue - blisters at hair bases

Ivy - colour pattern on leaf

Yellow-wort - glaucous

Wood Sage - rugose, veins much branched

Hoary Plantain - parallel veins

Astrantia - pink bracts below flowers

Red Clover - stipules

PLATE 8: FORMS OF FLOWERS

The diagram of a model flower shows the main structures present. The end of the flower stalk (pedicel) is called the receptacle and bears the other parts. A flower with its own stalk is called pedicillate, but one borne directly on the same stalk as other flowers is called sessile. The parts borne on the receptacle are typically in four sets (whorls) - from the outside inwards, sepals, petals, stamens and carpels. The forms they take are described in this and following plates.

Sepals, collectively called the calyx, are typically green.
Petals, collectively called the corolla, are typically of a colour other than green.
Stamens, collectively called the androecium, are the male reproductive organs. Each has a stalk called a filament and an anther at the top which contains many minute pollen grains, collectively known as pollen.
Carpels, collectively called the gynoecium, are the female reproductive organs. Each has an ovary at the bottom which is typically oval in shape and narrows at the top into a style, which ends in an area called the stigma, which is where pollen has to land if it is to fertilise the ovule inside the ovary.

Sometimes, sepals and petals have the same form, so that it looks like two sets of the same thing, when each structure is often called a tepal. Sometimes there is just one type of structure, which may be green like the model sepal or some other colour like the model petal, and usually labeled accordingly. Petals and sepals or tepals are collectively called the perianth.

Our model flower is radially symmetrical (or actinomorphic), in which any vertical cut through the centre produces at least roughly identical halves - as in Marsh Marigold (*Caltha palustris*), Green Hellebore (*Helleborus viridis*) and Fritillary (*Fritillaria meleagris*). This contrasts with bilaterally symmetrical (or zygomorphic), which means that there is only one vertical cut which produces identical halves, as in the two-lipped Wild Basil (*Clinopodium vulgare*) and Common Vetch (*Vicia sativa*) with one upright standard petal, two wing petals and two petals joined into a keel. Common Storksbill (*Erodium cicutarium*) can be either.

There are other whole-flower structures to consider. For instance, violets have, as well as “normal” flowers, small bud-like flowers which never open,. Some orchids have flowers which twist during their development so that they are upside down, while in Fritillary (*Fritillaria meleagris*) they hang upside down. Grasses and sedges, such as Upright Brome (*Bromopsis erecta/Bromus erectus*) and Hairy Brome (*Bromopsis ramosa/ Bromus ramosus*), have flowers without recognizable sepals and petals, consisting of stamens and carpels enclosed in various kinds of bract, the largest and outermost called glumes. In grasses the bracts often bear bristles called awns.

Structure of a typical flower

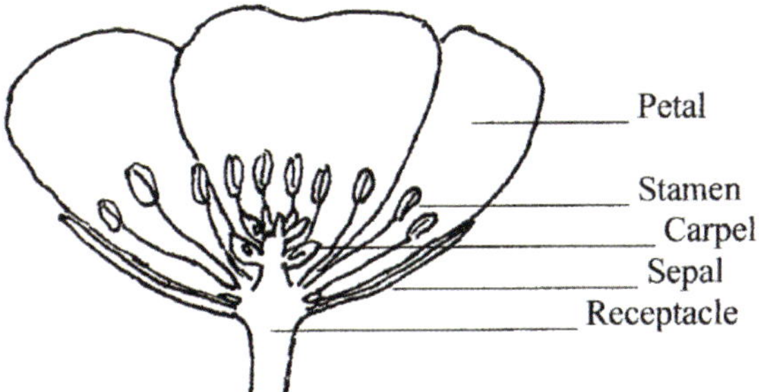

Fritillary - tepals 6, petaloid, upside down

Marsh marigold - perianth petaloid

Green Hellebore - perianth sepaloid

Wild Basil - zygomorphic, calyx and corolla tubular, 2-lipped

Common Vetch - zygomorphic, standard, wings and keel

Hairy Brome - flowers with glumes and awns

Common Storksbill - sepals and petals different

Upright Brome - stamens, stigmas and glumes

PLATE 9: VARIATIONS IN SEPALS

Sepals can vary in many ways. Their shapes have much in common with leaf shapes. They can be absent (as in grasses, shown in Plate 8), though this is difficult to know because of problems in distinguishing them from other structures. They can vary in number, or be joined to each other partially or entirely. They can invest the petals or be bent downwards (reflexed), as in Bulbous Buttercup (*Ranunculus bulbosus*). They can be longer, shorter or the same length as petals - Plate 8 shows them shorter in Common Storksbill, while they are longer in Field Pansy (*(Viola arvensis*). They can have a layer of bracts below them called an epicalyx, as in Musk Mallow (*Malva moschata*). They are affected, like petals, by whether the flower is actinomorphic or zygomorphic, as in Ground Ivy (*Glechoma hederacea*). They can take the form of a ring of hairs. They can be brightly coloured and perform the functions of petals. They can fall off the flower early or persist, sometimes remaining when the fruit is formed. Different sepals on the same plant can be different from one another, sometimes to make it look as though there is an upper and a lower lip. In Hairy St John's Wort (*Hypericum hirsutum*) they have stalked black glands on the margins.

Bulbous Buttercup - sepals reflexed,

Field Pansy - sepals free, longer than petals

Hairy St John's Wort - black glands on sepals

Musk Mallow - 5 sepals, 3 epicalyx segments

Ground Ivy - calyx tubular, some lobes longer than others

PLATE 10: VARIATIONS IN PETALS

Petals, and coloured tepals are even more varied. Like sepals, they can be absent (as in grasses, shown in Plate 8), or vary in number. They can have shapes found in leaves, be different colours or have different colours in different petals on the same flower or even within the same petal. They can be joined to each other partially or entirely or free. When joined the overall shape can be tubular, bell-shaped, urn-shaped or flat, or divided into two lips as shown for Wild Basil in Plate 8. When not joined, they can overlap each other or be clearly separate.

Illustrative photos here are of Marsh Arrowgrass (*Triglochin palustre*), Enchanter's Nightshade (*Circaea lutetiana*), Water Plantain (*Alisma plantago-aquatica*), Creeping Cinquefoil (*Potentilla reptans*), Yellow-wort (*Blackstonia perfoliata*), Foxglove (*Digitalis purpurea*), Harebell (*Campanula rotundifolia*) and Lily of the Valley (*Convallaria majalis*).

Marsh Arrowgrass - no petals

Enchanter's Night-shade - 2 bilobed petals

Water Plantain - 3 petals, separate

Creeping Cinquefoil 5 petals, separate

Yellow-wort - 8 -9 petals,

Foxglove - corolla wholly tubular

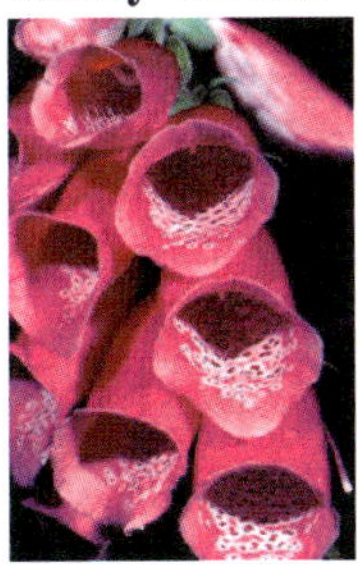

Harebell - corolla bell-shaped, 5 lobes

Lily of the Valley - urn-shaped, 6 lobes

PLATE 11: MORE VARIATIONS IN PETALS AND PETALOID TEPALS

Petals and petaloid tepals can be a variety of shapes, with much in common with leaf shapes. In many species a petal has a narrow basal part (the claw) and expands into a broader structure (the limb) at the top. Petals can be divided into two or more lobes (bifid, trifid, etc if the division is complete) or be indented at the top (emarginate). They can be inrolled, or wrinkled. They can be green or shiny or very small. Common St John's Wort (*Hypericum perforatum*) has black glands on the petals.

Differences between petals in the same flower are carried further than in sepals. They can differ randomly, be joined into a tube surrounding the inner flower parts, form upper and lower lips, often with a hood-shaped upper lip and a horizontal lower lip as a means of enabling particular insects to land and enter the flower. They can have hairs or colour patterns which also facilitate pollination by particular insects. Some petals can be different sizes and shapes from other petals. Common Milkwort (*Polygala vulgaris*) gets most of its colour from the sepals, but the lowest petal forms a remarkable fringed crest.

Petal characteristics have already featured in Plates 8 and 10. There are further examples here, using Black Mustard (*Brassica napa*), Water Chickweed (*Myosoton aquaticum*), Charlock (*Sinapis arvensis*), Great Hairy Willowherb (*Epilobium hirsutum*), Fennel (*Foeniculum vulgare*), Dewberry (*Rubus caesius*), White Deadnettle (*Lamium album*), Lesser Celandine (*Ficaria verna*), Common Milkwort (*Polygala vulgaris*), Moschatel (*Adoxa moschatellina*), Common St John's Wort (*Hypericum perforatum*), Field Bindweed (*Convolvulus arvensis*) and Hedge Woundwort (*Stachys sylvatica*).

Water Chickweed - 5 bifid petals

Black Mustard (left) and Charlock (right) - petals with claw and limb

Great Hairy Willow-herb - emarginate

Fennel - petals inrolled

Dewberry - petals wrinkled

White Deadnettle - lower lip and hooded upper lip

Lesser Celandine - petals shiny

Common Milkwort - petal a fringed crest

Common St John's Wort - black glands on petals

Moschatel - petals green

Field Bindweed - pink and white stripes

Hedge Woundwort - pattern on lower lip

PLATE 12: VARIATIONS IN STAMENS

Stamens, too, show many variations. They may be very numerous, few or absent, so that the flower is just female. The filament can be very long, or very short or absent and the anthers can be different shapes and in different numbers. Long stamens sometimes protrude from the flower, and then sometimes with slender, hanging filaments, as in Upright Brome in Plate 8. Some stamens can be different from others in the same flower, as in Great Mullein (*Verbascum thapsus*), where three of the anthers are placed horizontally on top of the filaments, the other two running down them vertically. Sometimes they can resemble petals. They can be separate from each other or joined together in a tube or otherwise, and can also be borne on the petals rather that the receptacle. Some stamens in a flower can be longer than others. Various outgrowths can appear on them. Sometimes the stamens take forms which do not allow their normal function, when they are called staminodes. They may, for instance, have no anthers. Stamens can have distinctive colours. In orchids, the stamens are replaced by ball-shaped clusters of pollen called pollinia, commonly concealed in a bag-like structure. More examples are to be shown in Plates 29-35.

Other plants used in the illustrative photos here are Black Bryony (*Tamus communis*), Germander Speedwell (*Veronica chamaedrys*), Opium Poppy (*Papaver somniferum*), Common Comfrey (*Symphytum officinale*), Black Nightshade (*Solanum nigrum*), Snapdragon (*Antirrhinum majus*), Common Figwort (*Scrophularia nodosa*) and Bee Orchid (*Ophrys apifera*).

Black Bryony - female flowers (no stamens)

Germander Speedwell - 2 stamens

Opium Poppy - stamens numerous

Great Mullein - 2 kinds of anther

Common Comfrey - stamens on petal tube, short filaments

Black Nightshade - 5 stamens, anthers joined into yellow tube

Snapdragon - stamens different lengths

Common Figwort - 4 anthers and staminode

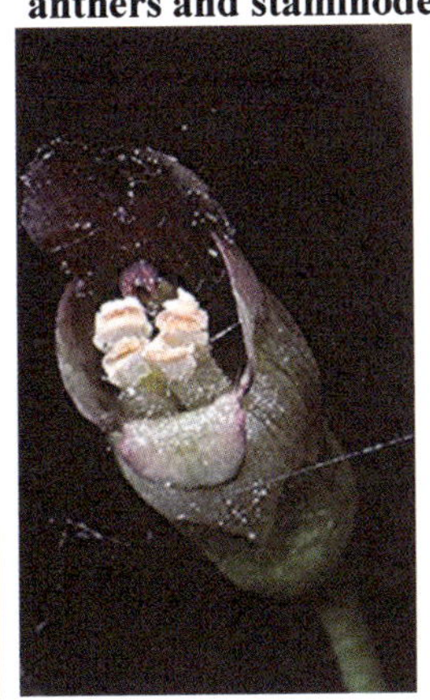

Bee Orchid - pollinium under hood

PLATE 13: VARIATIONS IN CARPELS

Carpels may be absent, so that the flower is just male There can be one, few or many. They can be separate or joined together in various ways to form a single ovary. Separate carpels can be oval, cylindrical or flattened, among other variations. When they are joined, the inside can have a single chamber or several and one or more ovules can commonly be seen inside if the ovary is opened. In ovaries formed from more than one carpel, the styles may join together into a single pistil or remain partially or entirely separate. Where they are joined, the stigma may still be divided into lobes. The stigmas can be brightly coloured. The ovary can be borne: above the insertion points of the other parts (superior ovary, hypogynous flower); below the insertion points of the other parts (inferior ovary, epigynous flower); round a hollow surrounding the insertion points of the other parts (superior ovary, perigynous flower).

Plate 12 showed a single superior ovary with a flat stigma with radial ridges in Opium Poppy, a single style in Black Nightshade and Common Comfrey and a single superior ovary with three bilobed stigmas in Black Bryony. Photos here feature another of Black Bryony (*Tamus communis*), Wood Anemone (*Anemone nemorosa*), Dog Rose (*Rosa canina*), Wallflower (*Erysimum cheiri*), Welsh Poppy (*Meconopsis cambrica*), Alpine Willowherb (*Epilobium anagall-idifolium*), Cherry Laurel (*Prunus laurocerasus*), Peach-flowered Bellflower (*Campanula persicifolia*) and Autumn Crocus (*(Crocus nudiflorus*).

Black Bryony - no carpels, male flower

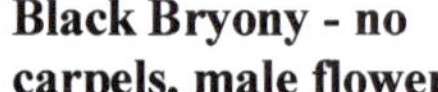

Wood Anemone - many separate carpels

Wallflower - superior, tubular, stigma bilobed

Dog Rose - carpels close together

Welsh Poppy - stigma 4-lobed

Cherry Laurel - superior, flower perigynous

Alpine Willowherb - inferior, tubular

Peach-flowered Bellflower - one style, stigma 3 lobed

Autumn Crocus - coloured stigmas

PLATE 14: TYPES OF NECTARY

Nectaries can be borne on any part of the flower - receptacle, petals, sepals or perianth segments, ovary, outgrowths from the stamens - or in separate tubular structures or downward growing pouches or spurs. Most contain a sugary liquid called nectar on which insects feed. Photos shown here are of Dogwood (*Cornus sanguinea*), Lesser Celandine (*Ficaria verna*), Snowdrop (*Galanthus nivalis*), Green Hellebore (*Helleborus viridis*), Columbine (*Aquilegia vulgaris*) and Fumitory (*Fumaria officinalis*)

Lesser Celandine - on base of petal

Dogwood - ring beside bases of petals

Snowdrop - green areas on tepal

Green Hellebore - separate tubular structures

Columbine - spurs

Fumitory - pouch

PLATE 15: TYPES OF INFLORESCENCE

Flowers are arranged in inflorescences. If all the flowers are at the end of the main stem above the foliage leaves, they form a single inflorescence. If more spread out, they are best regarded as separate inflorescences. The stalk of an inflorescence is called a peduncle, that of an individual flower a pedicel.

A simple raceme has a main axis which does not end in a flower. The flowers are on the ends of pedicels, which branch off the main axis singly. There may also be leaf-like structures called bracts on the axis, each immediately below a pedicel or at the base of the inflorescence. Sometimes the flowers are all or mostly on one side. A spike is a raceme with flowers borne directly on the axis, rather than stalked. In willows and poplars, the spike is called a catkin and often hangs downwards. A corymb is a raceme with its branches of different lengths so that all the flowers are on one level or form a uniform arc.

In a simple cyme, the main axis ends in a single flower and growth is continued by a branch, which then repeats the process - and so on. Any bracts present are opposite the flowers. If all the branches are borne on the same side in a spiral, it is called a helicoid or scorpioid cyme. In the stitchworts there are two opposite branches in succession to continue growth - a dichasial cyme.

A verticillaster has flowers in close clusters at each node with no or very short stalks. The cyathium, found in spurges), has a cup-shaped involucre bearing glands, an ovary on a stalk and several stamens representing male flowers.

Various types are shown here in Horse Chestnut (*Aesculus hippocastanum*), Wood Avens (*Geum urbanum*), Bluebell (*Hyacinthoides non-scripta*), Early Purple Orchid (*Orchis purpurea*), Goat Willow (*Salix caprea*), Wood Forget-me-not (*Myosotis sylvatica*), Greater Stitchwort (*Stellaria holostea*), Wild Cherry (*Prunus avium*), Yellow Archangel (*Lamiastrum galeobdolon*) and Sun Spurge (*Euphorbia helioscopa*). Further examples are in Plates 16 and 35.

Horse Chestnut - simple raceme

Wood Avens - simple cyme

Bluebell - one-sided raceme, bracts

Goat Willow - male catkins

Early Purple Orchid - spike

Wild Cherry - corymb

Wood Forget-me-not - scorpioid cyme

Greater Stitchwort - dichasial cyme

Yellow Archangel - verticillaster

Sun Spurge - cyathium with 4 glands

PLATE 16: MORE INFLORESCENCE TYPES

Inflorescences can be compound. A raceme of racemes is called a panicle. A corymb of corymbs is called a compound corymb. Umbels, where all the branches come off the main axis at the same point, are most commonly in groups with the umbel form, creating a compound umbel. A spike of spikes, notably in grasses, is confusingly called a spike and the component spikes called spikelets. In a compound umbel, the "bracts" at the base are labeled as bracts, but those in the component umbels are called bracteoles, and an inflorescence can have both, one or the other or none. Here, a single bract is shown in Fool's Watercress (*Apium nodiflorum*) and a ring of bracteoles but no bracts in Cow Parsley (*Anthriscus sylvestris*). If there is a separate stalk for the compound umbel, this is a peduncle. Guelder-rose (*Viburnum opulus*) has an umbel-like inflorescence with small fertile flowers in the centre and large sterile ones at the margin.

In some inflorescences, the component flowers are borne so close together as to look like a single flower. This is approached in Cow Parsley. It is taken further in the Daisy family (*Asteraceae*). Here the inflorescence is typically a capitulum, which has a flat or convex disc instead of an axis, all the flowers (called florets) being crowded together on it with a collection of overlapping bracts known as an involucre surrounding it. In Scentless Mayweed (*Tripleurosperm maritimum*) there are two distinct types of floret - a central disc of tubular yellow flowers (the disc florets) surrounded by a circle of radiating white flowers looking like petals (the ray florets). In Pineappleweed (*Matricaria discoidea*) all the flowers are disc florets, and in Hawkweed Oxtongue (*Picris hieracioides*) all ray florets. The involucres can sometimes be very hairy and sometimes spiny, as in thistles.

A variety of types of inflorescence, including capitula, are referred to as heads. The flowers are always stalkless or nearly so and clustered thickly together, so that little but the flower cluster is visible. The cluster can be cylindrical, conical, spherical or disc- or saucer-shaped. Bracts can be absent, associated with individual flowers or in a surrounding involucre.

Inflorescences can also differ in their positioning. In most plants they are either terminal or in the axils of leaves. In some members of the Parsley family (*Apiaceae*), however, each inflorescence is borne opposite to a leaf.

Photos here also feature False Oat Grass *(Arrhenatherum elatius*), Perennial Rye Grass (*(Lolium perenne*) and Chives (*Allium schoenoprasum*).

False Oat Grass - panicle

Cow Parsley - compound umbel, bracteoles, no bracts

Perennial Rye Grass - spike and spikelets

Guelder-rose - central and marginal flowers

Scentless Mayweed - capitulum, disc and ray florets

Pineappleweed - capitulum, disc florets only

Hawkweed Oxtongue - capitulum, ray florets only, involucre black

Chives - head, spherical

Fool's Watercress - leaf-opposed inflorescence

single bract

PLATE 17: TYPES OF FRUIT

When a pollen grain lands on the stigma of a flower, it fertilizes it, so that the ovule develops into a seed. Its protective outer wall is called the pericarp. The seed and pericarp are together called the fruit.

Fruits can be simple, aggregate or composite. A simple fruit is from a single flower with a single ovary containing one or more seeds, as in the legume of the pea family (*Fabaceae*) and narrow siliqua and broader silicula of the mustard family (*Brassicaceae*). An aggregate fruit is the collection of fruits formed from a single flower with more than one ovary, as in buttercups and Wood Anemone (*Anemone nemorosa*). A composite fruit is formed where individual fruits form a joint structure with other parts of the inflorescence, as in Wild Strawberry (*Fragaria vesca*), where they are partially embedded in the swollen receptacle.

A fruit may contain just one seed or any number. Where there are more than one, the fruit may have them all in a single internal space called a loculus, or it may be divided into 2 or more loculi, each containing one or a number of seeds. If there are two or more loculi, these most commonly run from bottom to top with dividing walls between them and usually join in the middle to form a central axis. Within a loculus, the seeds may be borne centrally or marginally.

Fruits can be dry or succulent, the latter incorporating soft material in addition to the seed to induce animals to eat the fruit to help in its dispersal. Several types of dry fruit have just one seed inside a protective layer called the pericarp, which ruptures under the pressure of the growing seed or decays to release it, so that it can be dispersed and grow into a new plant. These are often called achenes. If the pericarp is leathery or woody the achene becomes a nut. If the pericarp expands into a wing to aid dispersal of the fruit by the wind, it is a samara. In Pedunculate Oak (*Quercus robur*), the floral involucre of bracts becomes a cup in which the nut sits. Common Gromwell (*Lithospermum officinale*) has nuts with a hard, polished white outer covering.

Photos here include Common Vetch (*Vicia sativa*), Narrow-fruited Watercress (*Nasturtium microphyllum*), Honesty (*Lunaria annua*), Opium Poppy (*Papaver somniferum*), Beech (*Fagus sylvatica*) and Wych Elm (*Ulmus glabra*).

Common Vetch - legume

Narrow-fruited Watercress - siliqua

Honesty - silicula, outer walls removed

Wood Anemone - aggregate fruit of achenes

Wild Strawberry - composite of achenes on swollen receptacle

Opium Poppy - capsule, many seeds in several loculi.

Beech - nuts

Wych Elm - samaras

Pedunculate Oak - nut in cupule of bracts

Common Gromwell - shiny

PLATE 18: MORE FRUITS

Another general category of dry fruit is the capsular fruit, which contains many seeds and splits open in one of a number of ways to release them. If it splits down one side only it is called a follicle. If it splits along two opposite sides, it is a legume, silicula or siliqua. Legumes, siliquas and siliculas sometimes have a narrow terminal section called a beak. The last two have a central partition dividing the inside, with seeds either side, which a legume does not. Almost any other capsular fruit is called a capsule. Capsules may have a single internal chamber containing all the seeds or be divided into partitions, each with some of them, as in Opium poppy in Plate 17. Capsules open in a number ways, to be shown in Plate 36.

Yet another range of dry fruits are the schizocarps. Here the fruit splits into a number of segments still with their section of ovary wall. This can happen with some fruits which start off like legumes or siliquas and then break up transversely into one-seeded portions. In others, the fruit splits into segments from top to bottom. The unique example in *Geraniaceae* is shown in Plate 41.

Dry fruits can have other characteristics which distinguish one species from another, for instance, spiral, shiny, heart-shaped, ridged, beaked, warty and arranged like a bird's foot. In some species, the fruit just explodes (Plate 41). Plate 37 shows structures to aid dispersal by air, while Plate 39 shows some to help them attach to animals for dispersal.

Succulent fruits also take a variety of forms, to be shown in Plates 39 and 40. They are mostly fleshy, so that animals will eat them, and the fruits are embedded in the fleshy part. Blackthorn (*Prunus spinosa*) is an example.

Other examples illustrated here are Marsh Marigold (*Caltha palustris*), Black Mustard (*Brassica nigra*), Cow Parsley (*Anthriscus sylvestris*), Fool's Parsley (*Aethusa cynapium*), Black Medick (*Medicago lupulina*), Curled Dock (*Rumex crispus*), Wall Speedwell (*Veronica arvensis*), Birdsfoot Trefoil (*Lotus corniculatus*), Blackthorn (*Prunus spinosa*) and Dewberry (*Rubus caesius*).

Marsh Marigold - aggregate fruit of follicles

Cow Parsley - schizocarp separating into 2

Black Mustard - siliqua, beaked

Curled Dock - red warts

Fool's Parsley - ridged

Wall Speedwell - heart-shaped capsule

Black Medick- spiral

Birdsfoot Trefoil - legumes, bird's foot

Dewberry - aggregate of drupes, bloom

Blackthorn - drupe, blue bloom

PLATE 19: HOW FLOWERING PLANTS GERMINATE

Many plants produce a vast number of seeds to increase the chances of some germinating. Others produce fewer seeds but make them larger so that they have enough stored food to give them a good chance of germinating successfully before they run out of sustenance. Whatever the numbers, a seed must find a habitat in which it is possible for it to live, with temperature and water being within a range required for the species. Some require light to germinate, whereas others germinate only in darkness. Some species will germinate only after exposure to cold conditions for a period, while in others there is a period of dormancy before they will do so. Length of dormancy can vary within the same species, which means that some seeds can germinate as soon as suitable conditions occur, while others can remain dormant, sometimes for many years, as a reservoir in case no further seeds are produced. In other species, seeds will germinate continuously over a period of time, or in bursts with short intervals between.

Plants are made up of individual units called cells, which are usually too small to see with the naked eye. These cells divide and the daughter cells absorb water, which expands them to mature size, and then divide again. As more and more cells are produced, they develop differently according to the role they have to play in each part of the plant. A flowering plant typically starts life as a seed, which contains a group of not yet specialised cells called the embryo, which will grow into the plant, and stored food material to help it do so. The beginning of this process is called germination. The photos show three main germination patterns in flowering plants.

Sycamore (*Acer pseudoplatanus*) seeds abundantly, and sometimes a seed begins to germinate while still within the wall of the fruit. The radicle, or young root emerges first and grows down into the soil, developing branches. The seed either remains where it is or gets pushed into the air by elongation of the topmost part of the radical, called the hypocotyl. This is hooked to begin with, so that the seed is dragged upward rather than pulled, which makes damage less likely. In the process, the seed coat falls off and two simple leaf-like structures are revealed - the cotyledons or seed-leaves. They are at first folded and lying together, but eventually straighten and open out, revealing, between them a small shoot, the plumule. This grows rapidly and soon produces young but normal sycamore leaves. From there it gradually develops into the mature tree.

Yellow Flag (*Iris pseudacorus*) has a single cotyledon which remains inside the seed. The radical emerges first and grows down, eventually producing a root system. From where the radicle leaves the seed, a green structure grows upwards which is called the coleoptile. When it reaches a certain size, it becomes apparent that it is a sheath protecting the plumule, which eventually breaks through and grows into the mature plant.

Common Vetch (*Vicia sativa*) has both the radical and plumule emerging directly from the seed. First, the radical emerges and grows downwards and the plumule soon grows upwards from the radicle base and develops leaves with tendrils. The cotyledons remain within the seed and there is no sheath.

Sycamore (*Acer pseudoplatanus*) - stages of germination

Yellow Flag (*Iris pseudacorus*) - stages of germination

Common Vetch (*Vicia sativa*) - stages of germination

PLATE 20: THE INITIATION OF GROWTH

Plant growth involves the production of new organs throughout life. Indeed, almost any living plant cell is potentially capable of dividing to produce new cells, which can then develop to carry out specialised functions.

Firstly, the stems grow in length and width, and leaves and branches develop on them. Initiation of growth occurs in the stem apex which is usually enclosed in protective leaves forming a bud. Groups of cells called primordia, too small to be seen by eye, are formed in this growing stem apex, and get “left behind” on the sides of the stems as it grows. The left-behind primordia produce firstly leaves, then buds in the upper angles between leaf and stem called the axils. Some buds develop into branches. The area of the stem where a branch or leaf occurs is called a node and the areas between internodes.

Later, the stem apex produces, in many plants, further primordia which, when left behind on the sides of the stem, develop into leaf-like structures called bracts. Finally, the stem apex broadens to form the flower receptacle and groups of cells destined to grow into flowers - the flower primordia - develop on its sides or top. Within the flower primordia, a number of more specific primordia develop, destined to become sepals, petals, stamens and carpels.

Diagram to show stages of formation of primordia

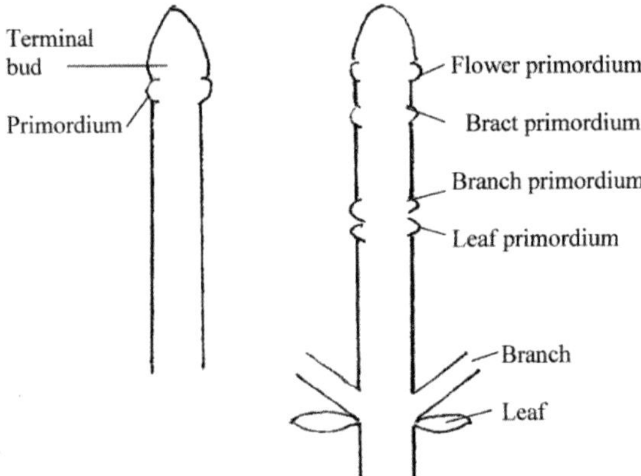

PLATE 21: HOW STEMS DEVELOP FOR SUPPORT

A stem supports all the other plant structures and houses a conducting system for water and nutrients. It must have strength, so that it does not collapse under its own weight or get knocked over by the wind or rain, competing plants or passing animals. Stems gain strength partly by the pressure of the water in their cells (turgor) and partly by tissues made of wood. The cross-section through a branch of an Ash tree shows how the whole of the centre of the tree is full of old wood. At the margins a protective layer of bark has formed, pierced by bordered pores called lenticels to allow oxygen and carbon dioxide to pass between the tissues and the air. Between the bark and the old wood is a layer of cells called the cambium which is too thin to be seen but which divides to produce xylem (young wood) on the inside and nutrient-conducting tissue called phloem and the protective layers on the outside. Each year a new layer of wood is laid down and these can be seen in the cut trunk of an Ash.

Most herbaceous plants have their supporting tissue in strands called vascular bundles, each with cambium producing phloem on the outside and xylem inside. These are usually either in a ring at the margin, where the main stresses on the stem occur, or more or less scattered throughout the stem. Placing a cut stem in a liquid food colorant or ink results in its being drawn up the stem through the vascular bundles or ring of xylem, so that, if the stem is cut across a little way from the bottom, the location of these structures can sometimes be seen. A protective surface layer called the epidermis also develops and is made up of cells with their outer surface covered with a fatty substance called cutin and often also wax which restrict loss of water and provide a protective firmness. Between the epidermis a range of different tissues arises which add to protection. The inner part of the stem is either composed of less specialized cells and called the pith or is hollow.

Ash (*Fraxinus excelsior*) - cross-section of trunk

Elder (*Sambucus niger*) - bark, lenticels

Cross-sections of stems placed in liquid food colorant -

Foxglove (*Digitalis purpurea*)

Yellow Flag (*Iris pseudacorus*)

PLATE 22: HOW ROOTS AND LEAVES DEVELOP FOR SUPPORT

As with stems, the growing point of a root is at its end, in this case the lowest part, and it is covered by a protective mucilaginous layer to minimize damage as it grows downward in the soil. The cells in the growing point divide and expand to form the various tissues of the mature root. The main functions of most roots are to hold the plant firmly in the soil and to absorb water and mineral salts from the soil for the plant's nutrition. They have the strengthening tissues at the centre to counteract forces that could pull them out of the soil. Early on, there is typically a star-shaped area of xylem there with areas of phloem between the points of the star. Both develop from a cambium between them as in stems. Gradually, the phloem is pushed outwards till there is a central core of xylem surrounded by a ring of phloem, just as in the stem of a tree. The central location can be seen in the cross-section of a root of Cow Parsley (*Anthriscus sylvestris*) which has drawn up liquid food colorant. The outer surface is protected by a covering called the exodermis and sometimes by corky cells. Small hairs (root hairs) project from the surface to absorb the water and mineral salts. Branches can also develop. Roots can develop in specialised ways or on unusual parts of the plant, as will be shown in Plates 23, 26 and 42.

Each leaf primordium develops into a protruberance on the side of the stem. Then it expands into the typical flattened form of the leaf, known as the lamina, most often narrowed where it joins the stem. A leaf sheath or stipules may develop at the base and the growth of a leaf stalk or petiole may separate the lamina from the stem. Within the leaf, veins develop as extensions of the vascular rings or bundles of the stem and support it. To do this effectively, they are usually distributed over its width and length in the ways shown in Plates 5 and 7. An impermeable outer layer prevents too much water loss but has tiny invisible pores called stomata, which can open to allow exchange of the oxygen and carbon dioxide necessary for nutrition or close to reduce water loss.

Cow Parsley - cross-section of root placed in liquid food colorant

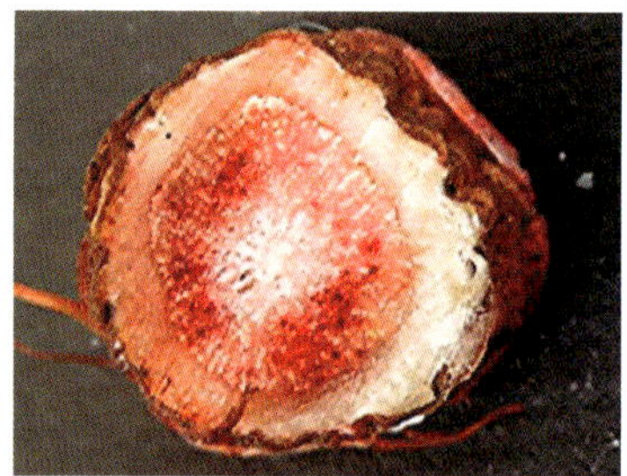

PLATE 23: ALTERNATIVE SUPPORT MECHANISMS

Some plants scramble over other plants for support, often with hooked hairs, prickles or thorns to increase their hold. Some climb up stronger plants or other firm objects, sometimes by twining round them, as in Greater Bindweed

(*Calystegia sepium*) and Black Bindweed (*Fallopia convolvulus*) and sometimes using specific devices, such as tendrils. White Bryony (*Bryonia dioica*) has tendrils which coil round parts of the supporting plant, each with two coils in the part between that and the Bryony stem, the upper and lower coils being in opposite directions, so that there is an abrupt change in the middle. This gives considerable elasticity, so that it yields to movements from the wind or other disturbance, rather than opposing them strongly and breaking. Virginia Creeper (*Parthenocissus quinquefolia*) has adhesive sucker-like discs at the tips of its branched tendrils. In vetches and peas, the tendrils replace leaflets and are either simple or branched. In Travellers Joy (*Clematis vitalba*), it is the leaf stalk which twines round the support, as will be shown in Plate 45. Ivy (*Hedera* helix) develops small roots on its stem to attach itself to a surface.

Bramble (*Rubus* - species) - prickles

Black Bindweed - twining stem

Greater Bindweed - twining stem

White Bryony - coiled tendril

Virginia Creeper - tendrils and suckers

Common Vetch (*Vicia sativa*) - leaf tendrils

Ivy - supporting adventitious roots

PLATE 24: GROWTH AND TIME

Growth is not normally continuous and uniform. In areas with a cold winter season it takes place mainly in spring and summer, when environmental conditions most favour it. In between, there are various devices for resting. Most plants produce seed, which is dormant and therefore requires very little energy and therefore little food. For annual plants, this is their main survival tactic. Biennial and perennial herbaceous plants often just have leaves or other structures near the ground during the unfavourable period to protect them against frost. In many of them, however, all or most of the above-ground parts die and the plant survives on food stored in mostly underground parts.

Storage organs are of various kinds. Some are underground stems called rhizomes, looking more like roots, though they are distinguished from them by having leaves or buds. Yellow Flag (*Iris pseudacorus*) has a thick rhizome growing horizontally and sending up a new season shoot at the end. Bulbous Buttercup (*Ranunculus bulbosus*) has a swollen stem base known as a corm. Corms are often mistakenly called bulbs - hence the name of this buttercup. A bulb, such as shown in the cultivated onion (*Allium cepa*), is also at the stem base, but is really a whole shoot base with the food stored mainly in the fleshy leaf bases. A vertical section shows the layers of fleshy leaves, which are not seen in a corm. In the spring, buds between the storage leaf bases develop into new shoots when favourable conditions return. A stem tuber is a swollen underground stem or part of a stem. In the potato, it is at the end of a branch, but in Cuckoo Pint (*Arum maculatum*) it occurs at the base of a main stem. Roots may also swell with stored food - Cow Parsley (*Anthriscus sylvestris*), like its cultivated relatives carrot and parsnip, has a swollen taproot. Orchids like *Dendrobium*, which we may have as house plants, have above-ground storage parts called pseudobulbs, which are thickened bulb-like stems for surviving dry periods.

Trees and shrubs have a different approach. They retain their aerial stems, which have a thick protective bark, and many of them shed their leaves (deciduous trees) and live on food material stored in the trunk or root. A winter twig of Horse Chestnut (*Aesculus hippocastanum*) shows the scars left where the leaves were shed and the buds it produces which develop into new shoots and leaves when favourable conditions return. Trees which retain their leaves over winter are called evergreen and their leaves are usually thick or waxy or hairy to protect against winter conditions.

Yellow Flag - rhizome

Bulbous Buttercup - corm

Onion - bulb cut in half

Cuckoo Pint - tuber

Horse Chestnut -

winter twig

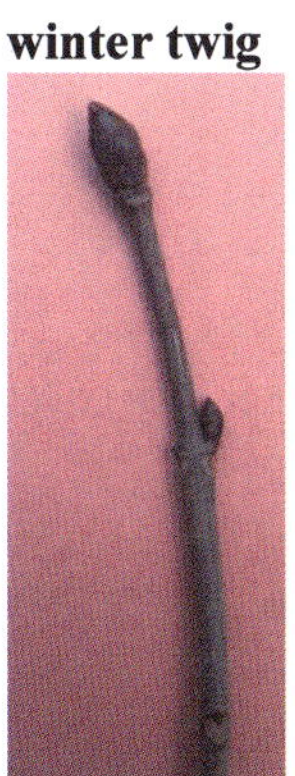

spring opening

***Dendrobium* species - pseudobulbs**

PLATE 25: HOW FLOWERING PLANTS PRODUCE AND USE FOOD

Leaves constitute the main food factory, manufacturing food substances from carbon dioxide from the air and water and mineral salts from the soil. This is done using the energy of sunlight and the process is facilitated (catalysed in chemical language) by the green pigment Chlorophyll, which occurs mainly in the leaves and accounts for their green colour. The first part of the process is called photosynthesis and produces energy-rich carbohydrates (sugars, starch, etc), and some of these are converted into fats and oils for energy and more into proteins for building materials by combination with mineral salts. The water and mineral salts are absorbed by the root hairs on the roots and travel through the plant via the xylem. It is believed that evaporation of water from the leaves draws water up these vessels as part of this process. The manufactured food substances are transported dissolved in water in the phloem to their required destinations.

Once food materials are manufactured the plant uses them for its life activities. The energy for them is obtained through the process of respiration, which can take place in any part of the plant. Respiration releases energy by breaking down carbohydrates into water and carbon dioxide by combining them with oxygen. The oxygen can be absorbed from the air by any part of the plant or from soil water by the roots or directly from the water in aquatic environments. The energy is used for growth by powering chemical reactions between carbohydrates and mineral salts to produce proteins, and to convert carbohydrates into other carbohydrates or into fats or oils. All of these can be used to build plant structures, which involves further chemical reactions which also utilize energy. Any excess of the types of foodstuff listed here can be put into storage in the plant and used later.

The exchange of materials between plant and environment and within the plants is illustrated in the diagram. Carbon dioxide can be obtained from the air for photosynthesis and oxygen for respiration. However, photosynthesis creates oxygen as a waste product and this can be used within the plant for respiration. Similarly, respiration has carbon dioxide as a waste product and this can be used within the plant for photosynthesis. This reduces the amount of exchange of gases needed with the air. Because photosynthesis cannot occur at night because it requires the energy of the sun, the plant will tend to absorb carbon dioxide and give out oxygen in the day and absorb oxygen and give out carbon dioxide at night. Within the plant, food produced by photosynthesis is transported to where building materials are needed or energy is required for the plant's living processes so that it can be the object of respiration.

The processes of food manufacture and use can produce waste products. There are various ways of getting rid of these, some not known. Many plants have glands, which are commonly spherical objects either directly on the plant surface - American Willow-herb (*Epilobium ciliatum*), shown in Plate 2, has these. Glands normally secrete substances, whose function is often unknown, but are likely to be waste products in some cases.

Only the most basic processes are covered here. Many other chemical substances are manufactured in the plant - plant hormones which travel through the plants carrying information about how cells or groups of cells should act, chlorophyll and other pigments which give colour to plants, enzymes which are chemicals which help chemical interactions of other chemicals, chemicals which produce smell and taste or are poisonous to deter feeding animals, and so on.

Exchanges involved in food manufacture and processing (excluding water)

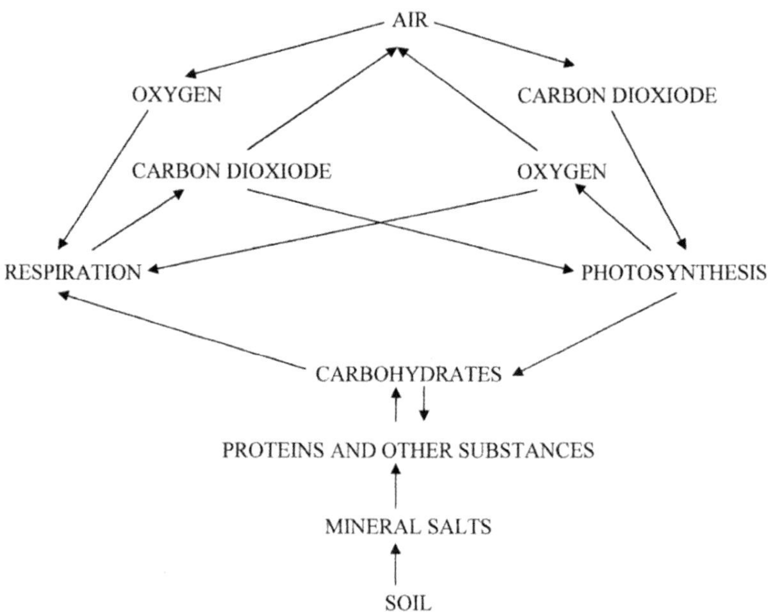

PLATE 26: ALTERNATIVE FORMS OF NUTRITION

Not all plants manufacture their own food and even those that do may supplement the processes described above by other methods.

Plants in the pea family (*Fabaceae*) have small bodies called root nodules attached to their roots which contain bacteria which can absorb nitrogen from the soil and turn it into nitrates to combine with carbohydrates to produce proteins. Bush Vetch (*Vicia sepium*) is an example.

A few plants can actually trap insects and absorb nutrients from their bodies. Sundews (such as *Drosera rotundifolia*) have sticky tentacles on their leaves to trap the insects, butterworts (such as *Pinguicula lusitanica*) have a sticky leaf surface which rolls up to enclose the prey, while Bladderworts (such as *Utricularia vulgaris*) have underwater bladders which draw insects in.

Plant parasites absorb their food from other plants instead of manufacturing their own, so do not photosynthesise, have no chlorophyll and are not green. Greater Dodder (*Cuscuta europaea*) is parasitic on nettles and other species. Dodders root in soil, and the elongating shoot makes exploratory spiral movements and coils round a nettle stem on contact. It then develops suckers or haustoria which penetrate the host tissues and absorb its tissues. The xylem and phloem fuse with those of the host, so that water and nutrients can flow from one to the other. The roots then die and the parasite is totally dependent on its host. If the host is an annual, the Dodder detaches itself when it has flowered and lives on its own reserves. If the host is perennial, contact is maintained. Common Broomrape (*Orobranche minor*) parasitises a variety of other species, but particularly clovers. Soon after germination, its roots attach themselves to the host's, penetrate it to reach the host vascular bundles and absorb all its nutrients from them. In the process it forms an underground tuber which is a channel for food transportation and from which flowering stems arise, often some distance away.

Mistletoe (*Viscum album*) is a partial parasite. It has indigestible seeds which pass through birds when they eat the succulent fruits and their droppings can infect a new tree. Birds also spread seeds when they wipe the sticky remains off their beaks on branches. They germinate on the branch of a suitable tree, such as Apple or Poplar, where the radicle forms an adhesive disc through which the root tip penetrates the host and connects with the host xylem and phloem to obtain food material. The aerial parts are green and carry out photosynthesis.

Birdsnest Orchid (*Neottia nidus-avis*) is a saprophyte, utilising the remains of living things in the soil. It has no chlorophyll because it makes no food of its own, and is a pale brown colour more or less throughout. Its root mass is an untidy ball consisting of a short rhizome surrounded by short stubby roots, both heavily infected with a fungus which absorbs food materials from the remains of dead animals and plants in the woodland floor. These pass into the orchid roots.

Bush Vetch - root nodules

Round-leaved Sundew - leaves with sticky tentacles

Pale Butterwort - leaves rolling up

Greater Bladderwort - bladders which trap insects

Greater Dodder

Greater Dodder - haustoria

Mistletoe - tree in fruit

Mistletoe - attachment

Common Broomrape - parasite, no green

Bird's-nest Orchid - saprophyte, no green

PLATE 27: HOW FLOWERING PLANTS MOVE AND REACT

We grow up believing that plants are passive things which stay where they are and have things happen to them. However, growth can be regarded as a form of movement. Moreover, plant stems generally grow in a kind of spiral oscillation rather than straight upwards. Such movements have already been described for Greater Dodder in Plate 26.

There are instances where it could be argued that the whole plant moves. In Brambles (*Rubus* species), for instance, the end of a long trailing stem may touch the earth, put down roots and form a new plant. The main difference from animal movement is in the time scale.

Many other movements are also growth movements but are more obviously induced by specific external stimuli. Movements towards or away from light are called phototropic movements. Thus a plant stem usually grows towards the light, and a root away from it. Most leaves grow to position themselves at right angles to the light falling on them. In Beech (*Fagus sylvatica*), the petiole grows as required to help to position the lamina so that it receives maximum sunlight.

Movements influenced by gravity are called geotropic movements. Place a stem in a horizontal position and it bends to grow upwards vertically. Roots, on the other hand, grow downwards. Growth movements can also be responses to contact (haptotropic or thigmotropic movements), as when the tendrils of a climbing plant coil round a stem which they touch, to chemical substances (chemotropic movements) or to water (hydrotropic movements). The radicles of seedlings, for instance, grow toward water and the plumules away from it.

Turgor movements are not produced by growth, but by changes in water pressure and do not occur in a specific direction dictated by the stimulus. Turgor can burst open some fruits, such as those of Indian Balsam in Plate 41. It also controls the opening and closing of the small pores in leaf surfaces through which oxygen, carbon dioxide and water vapour pass. Stinging Nettle (*Urtica dioica*) utilises turgor to defend itself by stings on its stem. A nettle sting is long and tapering with a broad rounded base whose contents are under pressure. When a nettle is touched the brittle end breaks off obliquely, producing a sharp point which punctures the skin and releases the pressure, which then forces the irritating contents into the wound.

A further range of specific non-directional movements may be brought about by differential growth or turgor or otherwise. The opening and closing of flowers in response to temperature or light is of particular interest and will be shown in Plate 28, along with other turgor movements in flowers. Other parts of the plant can also move in response to stimuli in some species. Sleeping Beauty (*Oxalis corniculata*) has its leaves lying in the same, more or less horizontal, plane by day but folded downwards at night. Old duckweeds (*Lemna minor*) absorb calcium from the water in autumn, which increases their weight so that they sink to the bottom, carrying the young shoots with them, where they avoid freezing. In spring the old plants decay and the young ones float back to the surface.

Bramble - shoot which has formed a root and grown a new shoot

Beech - laminas positioned to receive maximum sunlight

Stinging Nettle - stings

Sleeping Beauty - leaves horizontal by day

leaves folded at night

PLATE 28: HOW FLOWERING PLANTS REPRODUCE

Most flowering plants reproduce sexually. Male and female bodies meet and fuse to produce a fertilized ovum which grows into a seed, which is dispersed and then germinates. Many also, or instead, reproduce asexually. There are two main methods here. One is for new plants to form on vegetative organs such as roots or stems or even leaves and then become separated. This is called vegetative reproduction. The other method is for the female part of a flower to develop into a seed without any meeting with a male body. This is variously called parthenogenesis or apomixis or agamospermy. Sexual reproduction tends, on average, to produce healthier plants with more variations allowing growth in varied or changing environments. Vegetative reproduction allows rapid spread, with no wait for sexual processes to occur, and no dependence on unpredictable external agencies such as the wind or insects which are normally involved in the processes of sexual reproduction. It provides a plentiful supply of food for the new individual, whereas sexually reproducing plants supply only a small amount in the seeds. Some plants use both methods, benefiting from the advantages of both.

Sexual reproduction is carried out by the flowers. A typical flower has female structures called carpels which house the ovules and male structures called stamens. Part of the stamen is called the anther and contains many minute grains of pollen. The ovule and the pollen are the key players and they have to be brought together in some way. This is done by the anthers bursting open and transfer of the pollen to the stigma on top of a carpel or its style. Each pollen grain sends out a tube, too small to be seen even through a hand lens, which grows down the to the ovule, via the style where there is one, pierces it and fertilizes it, so that it can grow into a seed. These processes are called pollination.

Many plants have devices which protect the sexual reproductive parts. These include mechanisms which close the flower or inflorescence to protect it at night or in bad weather and reopen it when fertilization is likely and can be carried out safely. The sepals may move together to enclose the other parts, as in Lesser Celandine (*Ficaria verna*), whose open flower is shown in Plate 11, whereas in Common Daisy (*Bellis perennis*) the ray florets fold themselves inwards to protect everything inside them. A particular species will often close at particular times of day. Field Bindweed (*Convolvulus arvensis*) opens at about 5.00 am and closes at about 4.00 pm, but also closes at the approach of cloud and rain and opens only in warm and sunny weather. Goatsbeard (*Tragopogon pratensis*) has many tiny yellow florets in a head, which opens for only about an hour a day - roughly 10.00-11.00 am. This earned it the popular name Jack-go-to-bed-at-noon.

Lesser Celandine - flower almost closed

Common Daisy - head open

Common Daisy - heads closed

Field Bindweed - flower open

Field Bindweed - flower closed

Goatsbeard - head open

Goatsbeard - head closed

PLATE 29: METHODS OF POLLINATION

Transfer of pollen is brought about by two main agents - wind (anemophilous pollination) and animals, usually insects (entomophilous pollination). Many plants experience both, but some are almost entirely wind-pollinated, some almost entirely insect-pollinated. In a smaller number, transfer of pollen is by water - either it floats on the top or drifts underwater.

Pollen is very light and therefore easily carried by the wind. It must, however, be accessible to the wind, and so must the stigmas on which it needs to land. Many plants have stamens and stigmas which protrude and/or are not too crowded by other structures. Thus sepals and petals are commonly absent, and the flowers may be distant from leaves. Most British wind-pollinated trees flower very early in the year, before the leaves develop to get in the way of the wind, as in Hazel (*Corylus avellana*), whose male flowers are in drooping catkins and have only a small perianth and bracts at the base. The catkins are easily swayed by the wind, which helps the pollen to be thrown out. The female flowers are in groups and their long styles and dark red stigmas protrude to make them easily accessible to windborne pollen. In grasses the male flowers have stamens with long delicate filaments like Reed Canary Grass (*Phalaris arundinacea*), so that the anthers are easily shaken, and the female flowers have long feathery stigmas so that they easily catch passing pollen, as in Cord Grasses (*Spartina* species). Wind pollination requires the production and dispersal of very large amounts of pollen, since most of it will not reach a helpful target.

Plants pollinated by insects typically have colourful flowers and strong scents to attract them and sugary nectar or an abundance of pollen which they feed on. The attractive display is sometimes enhanced by large size of flowers and sometimes by clustering large numbers of flowers together, as in Ground Elder (*Aegopodium podagraria*). In the Dandelion (*Taraxacum* species) and its family (*Asteraceae*), the florets are all on the same base and look like a single conspicuous flower. Many other species in this family have conspicuous strap-like ray florets which attract insects and small tubular disc florets which produce seeds.

Different colours attract different insects - purples, blues and reds attract butterflies and larger bees, white and yellow other insects. Night-flying moths go for white or yellow, which are more conspicuous in dark conditions. Flowers visited mainly for feeding on pollen tend to be white, yellow or red. The colour is usually supplied by petals or sepals, but occasionally the stamens, as in Goat Willow (*Salix caprea*). The flowers of insect-pollinated plants must usually be shaped to allow the insect to land and to reach the nectar and pollen. Sometimes they just cling on, as in Aubretia (*Aubrieta deltoides*), sometimes there is a lip to land on, as in Yellow Archangel (*Lamiastrum galeobdolon*) and sometimes the flowers are aggregated to give a flat surface on which insects can walk about, as in Dandelion.

Hazel - stamens and stigmas accessible

Reed Canary Grass - long lax filaments protruding

Cord Grass - feathery stigmas

Ground Elder - large display

Hazel - abundant pollen

Dandelion - Orange-tip on flat top

Aubretia - bee clinging to flower

Goat Willow - bright yellow pollen

Yellow Archangel - bee on lip under hood

PLATE 30: SELF- AND CROSS-POLLINATION

If pollen is transferred from an anther to a stigma in the same flower, it results in self-pollination and self-fertilisation. Pollination of an ovule on one plant by pollen from a different plant is called cross-pollination and brings about cross-fertilisation. Transfer of pollen to a different flower on the same plant is often called cross-pollination, but it results in self-fertilisation. Some plants are habitually self-pollinated, some habitually cross-pollinated, and some can be pollinated either way. Cross-pollination increases the chances of cross-fertilisation, which promotes the creation of healthy offspring with more ability to adapt to a variety of changes in the environment than would be the case otherwise. If cross-pollination does not occur, self-pollination is the next best thing. Many plants therefore have pollination processes which allow self-pollination to occur if cross-pollination fails, so the species continues to exist.

Self-pollination is habitual in Shepherd's Purse (*Capsella bursa-pastoris*), which does it before the flowers open. Sweet Violet (*Viola odorata*) has cross-pollinating flowers early and later special flowers, which are tiny and buried among the leaves and never open. The pollen tubes grow through the anther wall and style to reach the ovules. The process is called cleistogamy, and looks like a fail-safe device to allow fertilization if cross-fertilisation has failed. In many other species, self-pollination occurs in an open flower. This is habitual in Bee Orchid (*Ophrys apifera*). The early upright position of its pollinia is shown in Plate 12. Later, the pollinia come forward out of their pouches and dangle in front of the stigmas. A breath of wind is likely to blow them against the stigmas, when pollination occurs.

Cross-pollination is the norm in many plants. Hogweed (*Heracleum sphondylium*) has its stamens ripening before the stigmas become receptive (called protandry), so that self-pollination can occur only in the overlap stage. The ovary has a shiny, horizontal, disc-shaped nectary on its very top. The secreted nectar simply lies on this surface, where any insect can reach it and both anthers and stigmas are readily accessible. The stamens are at first in the centre of the flower with their filaments curved inwards. Each stamen in turn elongates and straightens its filament, so that the anthers move to the edge of the flower and face upwards, where they shed pollen which easily brushes off on to visiting insects. During this time, the two stigmas are pressed together and unreceptive and only when the stamens fall off do the stigmas curl out to receive pollen.

Blackthorn (*Prunus spinosa*) has the stigma ripe before the stamens, which is called protogyny. Insects visit both for pollen and for the nectar which collects in the cup formed by the petals. When the flowers open, the stamens are curved strongly inwards and the style, and thus its stigma, projects beyond them and is therefore the first part to be touched by a visiting insect, which may then cross-pollinate them. Later the stamen filaments elongate and the anthers spread upwards and outwards, and produce pollen. Its position is far from the stigma, which may be carried further away by growth of the style, so insects can collect pollen without touching the stigma.

Sweet Violet - plant with normal flowers

cleistogamous flower

Hogweed - flowers at male stage

flowers at female stage

Bee Orchid - flower with drooping pollinia

Blackthorn - flowers with most anthers curved inwards and most anthers curved outwards

PLATE 31: DEVICES FAVOURING CROSS-POLLINATION

Devices to promote cross-pollination are sufficiently common in well-known flowers to be grouped, for description, as:

- anthers and stigmas ripening at different times;
- male and female flowers ripening at different times;
- male and female flowers on separate plants;
- designs which fit flower characteristics to the form of pollinating insects;
- bilaterally symmetrical designs allowing complex pollination mechanisms;
- designs to fool insects into pollinating without benefit;
- whole inflorescences designed for complex pollination mechanisms.

Plate 30 has featured flowers in which anthers and stigmas ripen at different times. Cross-fertilisation is made even more likely by having separate male and female flowers which are ready for pollination at different times. In Beech (*Fagus sylvatica*), for instance, the female ripen first (protogynous flowers). In Red Campion (*Silene dioica*) male and female flowers are borne on different plants, making cross-pollination inevitable except when bisexual flowers occasionally occur. The male flower has ten stamens in two whorls of 5, with a nectar ring at the base and the anthers at or protruding from the mouth of the petal tube. The female flower has a single ovary surrounded by a nectar ring at the base and surmounted by 5 styles which reach or exceed the mouth of the tube. Plates 12 and 13 have shown Black Bryony with male and female flowers on different plants.

Flowers pollinated by short-tongued insects, such as beetles and flies, do not require elaborate adaptations of their flower structure. Plate 30 has already shown how flowers such as Hogweed and Blackthorn rely on the stamens and stigmas ripening at different times to promote cross-pollination. In both of these, the insect can go straight to the nectar, with no constraints on its movement. Wood Anemone (*Anemone nemorosa*), however, does control insect movements to some extent. The stamens ripen first and are initially crowded over the stigmas to prevent too early access to the stigmas and prevent pollen reaching them while it is shed only from the outer stamens. Later, the stamens diverge so that the stigmas are more easily visited. Less evidently, the stigmas will not accept pollen from the same plant.

Beech - male and female inflorescences

male inflorescence

female inflorescence

Red Campion - female flower from above

female flower cut in half

male flower from above

Red Campion - male flower cut in half

Wood Anemone - stamens over stigmas

Wood Anemone - stamens diverging

PLATE 32: CROSS-POLLINATION BY BEETLES, FLIES, HOVERFLIES, SHORT-TONGUED BEES AND WASPS

A very large number of flowering plants have flowers shaped so that the insect receives pollen on a particular part of its body, which is most likely to brush first against the stigma of the next flower visited. This may be brought about by making the insect land on the flower or enter it or probe into it to find nectar in particular ways. Such flowers usually have the petals upright and forming a tube either by overlapping or being physically joined. The photograph of Astrantia (*Astrantia major*) shows a bee inserting its proboscis into a flower of this type to reach nectar.

In Greater Stitchwort (*Stellaria holostea*), the nectar is in globular nectaries at the base of the stamens, and can be reached only by tongues at least 3mm long, a length attained by the species of flies, beetles and bees which visit it. Its petals overlap, but allow fairly easy access. The anthers and stigmas are near the mouth of the flower, and the insect brushes against both stigmas and anthers as it probes, giving opportunities to collect or provide pollen. The anthers are ripe before the stigmas, which are pressed together at this stage and so unable to receive pollen. As the stamens wither, the stigmas open and curve outwards to maximize the chance of receiving pollen. Cross-pollination is, therefore, likely to occur sometimes. There can, however, be overlap between ripeness of stigmas and anthers, so that self-pollination can occur, especially as the outward bending of the stigmas brings them into contact with the withering stamens.

Primrose (*Primula vulgaris*) has both sepals and petals joined into tubes and only an insect with a tongue at least something like 6mm long, such as bees and beeflies, can reach the nectar secreted round the base of the ovary. The stamens are borne on the petal tube rather than on the receptacle, which allows special positioning. There are two types of flower borne on different plants. One type of flower, called thrum-eyed, has the stamens at the mouth of the tube, with the style being short, while the other, called pin-eyed, has a long style with the stigma at the mouth of the tube and the stamens further down. So when an insect pokes its tongue into the flower, it collects pollen on the base of its proboscis in a thrum-eyed flower and the middle of its proboscis in a pin-eyed. Transfer of pollen to a stigma normally occurs only when it is at the level of the stigma, which will happen only in a flower of the opposite type from that from which the pollen was collected. Accidental pollination by the same type of flower is prevented also because the texture of the stigma surface is different in the two types in a way which makes it difficult for pollen from the same type to lodge on it. In Purple Loosestrife (*Lythrum salicaria*) there are three different positions.

Astrantia - bee inserting proboscis

Greater Stitchwort - flower dissected to show stamens

Greater Stitchwort - dissected to show ovary and stigmas

Primrose - pin-eyed and thrum-eyed flowers from above

Primrose - pin-eyed section

thrum-eyed section

PLATE 33: CROSS-POLLINATION BY LONGER-TONGUED BUMBLE BEES, BUTTERFLIES AND MOTHS

The even longer tongue of butterflies, moths and the larger bees is required for effective cross-pollination of some flowers. Plate 32 showed a bee penetrating an Astrantia flower with its long proboscis. Some flowers, such as Red Campion (*Silene dioica*) and Yellow Flag (*Iris pseudacorus*), require a tongue of perhaps 10-12mm length, which is held to exclude everything except butterflies and moths, of which the latter carry their long tongues coiled up in a spiral under the head when flying. Plate 31 showed the calyx with its five petals united into a strong tube which holds the free petals in tubular form in Red Campion. This allows access to the nectar at the base only by a long tongue. Each petal has a terminal flap which partly closes the mouth to deter small insects from creeping in and helping themselves to the nectar. Butterflies and bumble bees reaching the nectar receive pollen from the anthers or dust it on to the stigmas, but self-pollination is impossible because of the separate male and female flowers.

Yellow Flag (*Iris pseudacorus*) has "revolver flowers", with a ring of three narrow tubes, all leading to nectar and shaped in a way which brings about pollination. The perianth has 6 yellow segments joined into a tube below and arranged in two whorls. The segments of the conspicuous outer whorl have broad drooping lobes spotted with orange and bearing markings to attract and guide the bees to the nectar. Those in the inner whorl are erect with incurved tips. The single style divides into three yellow arms which are broad and look like petals and spread sideways immediately over the perianth lobes. The three stamens lie between the perianth lobes below and the stylar arms. Each stylar arm has a narrow ridge and projection near the end which forms the stigma. A bumble bee or hoverfly lands on one of the outer perianth lobes and its weight pushes it down, allowing access to the flower. As it enters to reach the nectar in the perianth tube, its head comes into contact with one of the three stigmas and cross-pollinates it if it already carries pollen. Further probing brings its head and back against the anther where it collects pollen to transport to another flower.

Many plants pollinated by long-tongued insects are bilaterally symmetrical to promote complex pollination mechanisms. In the radially symmetrical flowers shown so far, the insect can enter the flower at any point and any way round. Bilateral symmetry, in contrast, allows devices which prescribe exactly how the insect will enter the flower. The stamens and stigmas can then be positioned more precisely to ensure contact with the right part of the insect at the right time. Foxglove (*Digitalis purpurea*) has joined petals forming an elongated bell which hangs obliquely downwards, shown in Plate 10. It is visited chiefly by bumble-bees, who are attracted by the purple colour and guided by the white blotches on the lower inside surface of the flower. Their bodies fit closely into the bell with their backs against the upper side of the flower while they probe for nectar, which is in a yellowish ring round the base of the ovary. Its back comes into contact with the anthers of the four stamens and becomes dusted with pollen. At this stage, the top of the style is upright against the corolla tube surface and does not normally touch the bee, and the two lobes of its stigma are pressed close together and so cannot have pollen deposited on them. Later, the style leans forward into the tube and the stigma lobes diverge so that bee carrying pollen from another flower dusts it on the stigma. At this stage, the stigma and anthers are very close together, so self-pollination can also occur.

Yellow Flag - flower from above

flower from the side

Yellow Flag - stylar arm from below, stigmatic ridge, stamen

flower cut in half to show perianth tube and inferior ovary

Foxglove - two views of flower cut in half to show male and female organs

PLATE 34: OTHER POLLINATION MECHANISMS IN BILATERALLY SYMMETRICAL FLOWERS

Yellow Archangel (*Lamiastrum galeobdolon*) has a corolla tube with a lower lip which juts out to form a landing platform for the pollinating bees and an upper lip which protects the reproductive structures. There are four stamens, two long and two short, whose anthers are under the upper lip and the single style terminates in a forked stigma, also under the hood. The bee alights on the lower lip and, guided by the reddish brown markings on it, forces its head (if a bumble-bee) or most of its body (other kinds of bee) into the flower to reach the nectar secreted from a ridge at the base of the ovary, as shown in Plate 29. Its back touches the anthers which project towards it, but the style is pressed against the hood out of reach. At a later stage, the style bends forward so that the stigma touches the bee's back at the spot where it received pollen. Cross-pollination is the most likely outcome. A ring of hairs inside the corolla tube keeps out smaller insects which might steal the nectar.

Common Toadflax (*Linaria vulgaris*) has a similar pollination mechanism, but its mouth is closed. Only the strong hive and bumble-bees bees can prise it open. The bee is guided to the spot to exert pressure by a dark yellow or orange area and lands on the lower lip to do it. The nectar collects in the spur which continues downwards from the corolla tube.

Honeysuckle (*Lonicera periclymenum*) has a very long corolla tube and only moths with tongues perhaps 30mm or more long can reach nectar at the end of it, though the nectar can collect in the tube to be more accessible. At first opening, the flowers are glowing creamy white and have a powerful scent. The anthers protrude from the corolla tube on long filaments and split open to release the pollen as evening approaches. The style is bent down out of the way, so the anthers are the first parts of the flower to be touched by the moth, which has pollen brushed on to it. The following day, the he style bends upwards so that it is hit by the moth first and can receive pollen from another flower.

Birdsfoot Trefoil (*Lotus corniculatus*) differs from other examples here in that the stamens and style come into contact with the underside of the insect. The easily visible parts are a conspicuous vertical standard petal marked with guiding red lines and two horizontal petals called wings. The wings lie close together and enclose the keel, which is two petals joined with a small opening at the end. It houses 10 stamens, nine joined into a tube within the keel, the uppermost one free and standing apart, and the style and stigma. Pollen is shed while still in bud, but when the flower opens, the filaments of 5 stamens swell, pushing pollen towards the keel opening. When a bee visits and probes to reach the nectar secreted at the base of the flower, its weight presses on the wing and keel petals which causes the stigma to act as a piston and push pollen out of the keel's terminal opening, so that it comes off on the insect's underside. Later the stigma protrudes through the hole and can be pollinated by insect visitors.

Yellow Archangel - flower with two lips

section to show style and a stamen

Common Toadflax - flower

Honeysuckle - ripe stigma stage

Birdsfoot Trefoil

Birdsfoot Trefoil -

keel revealed

stamen tube and free filament revealed

more of stamens revealed

PLATE 35: SOME PARTICULARLY REMARKABLE POLLINATION MECHANISMS

Pyramidal Orchid (*Anacamptis pyramidalis*) has a flower with six perianth segments. Three of these curl over to form a hood, two others are curved and spreading, while the sixth is a three-lobed downward-sloping lip prolonged backwards into a slender curved spur. At the entrance to the spur is an upright structure called the column. Adhering to the column are two club-shaped masses of pollen known as pollinia. Each pollinium has a stalk and the two stalks are joined to a single narrow strap below and covered by a flap. On the sides of the column just above the spur mouth are two roundish areas which are the stigmas. The flower is visited by butterflies and day and night flying moths, especially burnet moths. The scent is strong and sweet by day and unpleasant by night. The insect's objective is to suck the sap from the walls of the spur. It lands on the lip, unrolls its long proboscis and pushes it into the mouth of the spur, guided by two vertical ridges along the lip. The proboscis pushes back the flap over the pollinia and the sticky disc which joins them at the base wraps itself round the proboscis, sticks there and hardens into a cement. This action also moves the pollinia slightly further apart. As the insect flies away in search of another flower, the two pollinia move forward, so that, when they visit the next flower, they will hit the stigmas and bring about pollination. The process can be watched by inserting the tip of a needle to collect the pollinia and seeing what happens to it. As many as eleven pollinia can be collected on the same proboscis from successive visits to different flowers - a huge supply.

Fly Orchid (*Ophrys insectifera*) has a flower that looks like a species of wasp. Males of that species mistake it for a female, try to copulate with it (pseudocopulation) and pollinate the flower in the process. The more dramatic mimicry of the Bee Orchid probably relates mostly to its past history, since it is normally self-pollinated in Britain, as shown in Plates 12 and 30.

Cuckoo pint (*Arum maculatum*) has a pollination mechanism involving the inflorescence as a whole. It consists of a flower spike called a spadix topped by a purple column and enclosed in a green sheath called a spathe. The flowers are arranged on the lower part of the spadix. The female flowers are at the bottom, consisting only of ovaries topped by stigmas, and male flowers are above them, consisting of short-stalked stamens. The female flowers ripen first. The spadix emits a nasty smell which attracts mainly dung-frequenting flies. They land at the spathe opening and fall off it and into the chamber containing the flowers. Hairs at the top let the insects fall through but not fly out again, and the surfaces of spathe and spadix below these hairs have downward-pointing projections which prevent their climbing up them. So they fly around inside for about two days, sometimes in thousands, pollinating the female flowers with pollen from another plant. Soon the male flowers become mature and the insect becomes dusted with their pollen. The hairs at the top shrivel and the surface of the spadix changes so they can climb out and fly off to pollinate a plant in its female phase.

Pyramidal Orchid - flower spike

flowers with ridges and column

flower with ridges and flaps concealing pollinia

lip removed to show stigmas and pollinia in flaps

pollinia at removal

pollinia a minute or two later

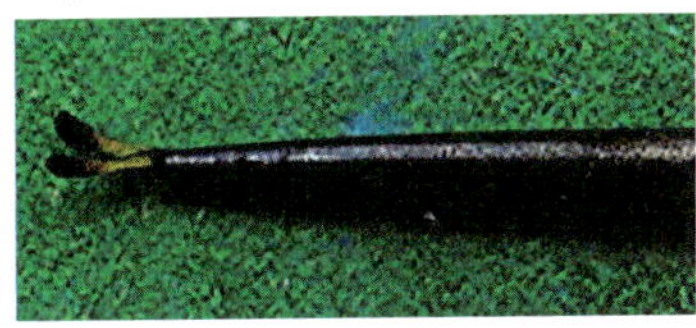

Fly Orchid - flower resembling wasp

Cuckoo pint - spathe and top of spadix

spathe cut away to show the flowers

PLATE 36: DISPERSAL OF FRUITS BY WIND

The fertilized ovule develops into a seed, and the seed and its protecting ovary wall are together called a fruit. For reproduction to be completed, these seeds have to be dispersed to places where they can germinate and grow into new plants. These places need to be some distance from the parent plant to give the seedlings a better chance of survival through not having to compete with the parent for food, light, water, etc. Dispersal can occur in many ways, but the commonest are wind, water, animals and forcible ejection. This can apply to fruits or seeds, since fruits are sometimes dispersed without prior release of the seeds and sometimes the seeds escape and are dispersed.

The seeds of some plants, such as orchids, are so small and light that they are easily blown about by the wind. Others have special devices to aid the process. Firstly, the fruit may open in a way that allows seeds to escape only when the wind is blowing strongly. This is the case with poppies, where the capsule has holes around the top through which the seeds are thrown out when the fruit is blown to one side, as already shown in Plate 17, and Nettle-leaved Bellflower (*Campanula tracheliums*) which has the holes at the bottom. Others develop a number of vertical slits, all along the sides in the follicles of Marsh Marigold (*Caltha palustris*), shown just beginning to open in Plate 18 and fully open here, and the capsules of Hoary Willowherb (*Epilobium parviflorum*). In the capsules of Spiked Star of Bethlehem (*Ornithogalum pyrenaicum*) they are part way down the sides. Some have a hinged opening lid, such as Scarlet Pimpernel (*Anagallis arvensis*) and some split into segments which separate, as in Yellow Flag (*Iris pseudacorus*). In Cowslip (*Primula veris*), the flowers are drooping at maturity but, by the time the capsule is ripe, have moved into an upright position so that the dry seeds are shaken out of the openings at the top only when a wind blows.. The persistent calyx which holds on to the seeds in Yellow Rattle (*Rhinanthus minor*) may be a way of keeping them on the plant till they are mature.

Nettle-leaved Bellflower - capsule, basal opening

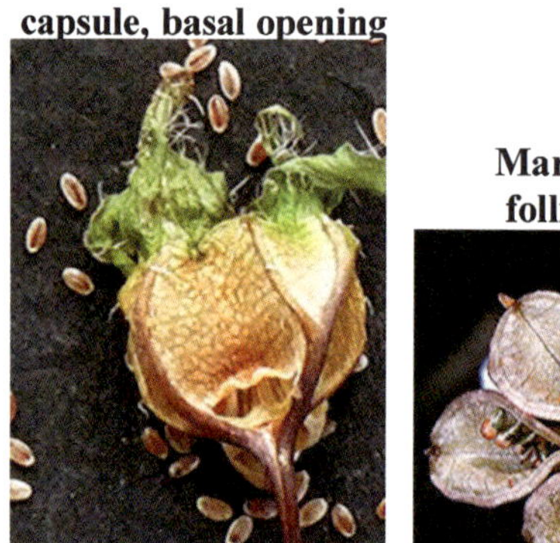

Marsh Marigold - follicles open

Hoary Willowherb - capsule, vertical slits, plumed seeds

Scarlet Pimpernel - capsule with hinged lid closed and opening

capsule with hinged lid open and seeds shed

Spiked Star of Bethlehem - capsule with slits partway

Yellow Flag - capsule segmented

Cowslip - flowers drooping

capsules upright

Yellow Rattle - persistent calyx enclosing seeds

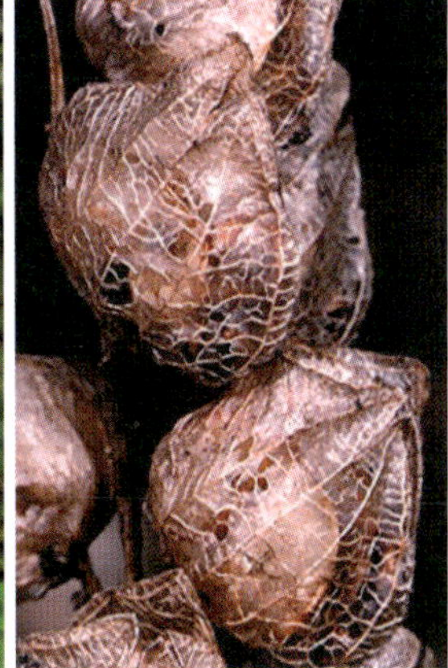

PLATE 37: DEVICES FOR STAYING IN THE AIR

In many plants, wind-dispersed seeds or fruits have structures which offer resistance to the wind so that the fruits take longer to fall to the ground, so that they may be dispersed further. Some have the fruit entirely flattened like Honesty (*Lunaria annua*), shown in Plate 17, while others have flattened wings like Wild Angelica (*Angelica sylvestris*). In samaras, the wing is large, as in Wych Elm (*Ulmus glabra*), shown in Plate 17. In Ash (*Fraxinus excelsior*), the wing has a twist, giving a propeller effect. In Sycamore (*Acer pseudoplatanus*), there are two samaras joined together which usually separate on dispersal. In limes, the fruits are attached to a large flattened bract. Seeds have flattened wings in Yellow Rattle (*Rhinanthus minor*).

Another set of flotation devices is produced by hairs in various arrangements to make "parachutes". The arrangement in dandelions is well-known. Each achene is surmounted by a pappus of hairs on the end of a long stalk, and the whole collection of fruits on a head is then in the form of a sphere which can float in the air. The spheres also break up and the individual fruits can then be carried some distance with the aid of their parachutes. The hairy style on the end of each fruit of Old Man's Beard (*Clematis vitalba*) is another example. The fruits with their plumes are in groups on a common stalk and come close together in wet weather, separating to become exposed to the wind in dry weather when they are lighter and less likely to adhere to other wet vegetation and can therefore be dispersed further. In Red Valerian (*Centranthus ruber*), the calyx becomes a bell-shaped feathery pappus. In willowherbs the seeds bear the parachutes, as shown in Plate 36. Each plume has many silky hairs. In damp conditions these shrink and the parachute clamps up so that it is not easily dispersed. In warm dry air it opens and is more likely to be dispersed. In the Bulrush (*Typha latifolia*) each spike, which may contain 117,000 to 268,000 tiny seeds, bursts at maturity, releasing the fruits in a fluffy cloud.

Ash - samaras with twist in wing

Wild Angelica - schizocarps with wings

Sycamore - two joined samaras

Large-leaved Lime - nuts, flattened bract

Old Man's Beard - achene, feathery style

Yellow Rattle - seeds with flattened wings

Dandelion - part of sphere of plumed achenes

Red Valerian - capsules with parachutes

Bulrush - seeds with parachutes

PLATE 38: WATER DISPERSAL

Some water plants flower and fruit underwater and the fruits are carried by currents to where they can root and grow into new plants. Others bear flowers above water, but the fruits may fall into it and be swept away. With heavier seeds which might sink too quickly for efficient dispersal, the seeds or fruits sometimes have spongy attachments with air pockets to make them buoyant, as in Yellow Waterlily (*Nuphar lutea*), whose berry breaks up and floats away. The fruit wall eventually decays and allows the seeds to sink and germinate. Yellow Flag (Iris *pseudacorus*) has air pockets in the seed coata. This gives them a spongy texture, which enables the seeds to float for at least 7 months.

Yellow Waterlily - berry

Yellow Flag - spongy seed coat

PLATE 39: ANIMAL DISPERSAL

Seeds and fruits are dispersed by animals by adhering to them, being carried away or being eaten. Adherence is helped by hooked spines. These are borne on the achene wall in Enchanter's Nightshade (*Circaea lutetiana*). In Wood Avens (*Geum urbanum*), the achene styles persist and are hooked. In Early Forget-me-nots (*Myosotis ramosissima*) the hooks are on the calyx, which is dispersed with the seeds. Blackjack (*Bidens pilosa*) has forked spines on the achenes. Great Burdock (*Arctium lappa*), has hooked bracts on the flower head so that the whole head is carried off. Fruits and seeds may also become sticky when wet and stick to animals for dispersal, as in Groundsel (*Senecio vulgaris*).

Fruits and seeds can, alternatively, be eaten or carried off to be eaten, and this often helps dispersal. Nuts from Hazel, Beech or Oak may be dropped on the way or buried for future use and not reclaimed. Seeds of Common Daisy (*Bellis perennis*) are taken off by ants to eat, and some discards may germinate where they are left. In many cases, however, the fruit is succulent and only the succulent part is eaten and the seeds discarded. Some birds overeat and are then sick, bringing up the seeds or fruits some distance from the parent. In Mistletoe (*Viscum album*), the bird which eats the berry may wipe its beak clean on the branch of a suitable host tree and deposit the seed where it can germinate.

Succulent fruits are divided into named types. Wild Plum (*Prunus domestica*) has a drupe, in which one or more seeds are surrounded by a hard stone with the succulent part surrounding it. Cuckoo Pint (*Arum maculatum*) and Bittersweet (*Solanum dulcamara*) have berries, which are more or less pulpy throughout, with the seeds embedded in the pulp without separate covers. Rowan (*Sorbus aucuparia*) has a pome, which consists of an enlarged fleshy receptacle with the fruits inside it, as in apples and pears.

Enchanter's Nightshade - hooked spines

Wood Avens - hooked styles

Early Forget-me-not - hooked bristles on calyx

Blackjack - achenes with forked spines

Great Burdock - hooked bracts

Wild Plum - drupe whole and cut in half

Bittersweet - unripe berry whole and cut in half with perhaps 7 seeds

Rowan - pome whole and cut in half

PLATE 40: MORE ON ANIMAL DISPERSAL

In some cases of animal dispersal the seeds have a succulent attachment sought by animals, who then disperse them. Spindle (*Euonymus europaea*) has 4 pink lobes, which are the fruit walls and surround white seeds, and an orange fleshy attachment to the seed called an aril to attract birds. Red Deadnettle (*Lamium purpureum*) seeds have oil-filled attachments which attract ants. Stinking Hellebore (*Helleborus foetidus*) has attachments which attract snails.

Colour is sometimes helpful in animal dispersal, as in Spindle. The fruiting inflorescence of Wayfaring Tree (*Viburnum lantana*) can be seen to have drupes of three different colours - green, red and black. These represent stages in maturity of the fruit and birds ignore the green and red and attack the black, thus preventing wastage of unripe fruit. Woody Nightshade (*Solanum dulcamara*) has them changing from green to yellow to orange to red and also a change of taste from bitter at first and then sweet - hence its other name of “Bittersweet”.

Humans also contribute to fruit dispersal. They may brush against plants to cause movements which throw out seeds which are then dispersed by the wind. Hooked fruits may cling on to them and be dropped elsewhere. One botanist raised 300 plants of 20 different species from the dirt inside his trouser turn-ups. Children’s (and indeed adults’) games with the adherent fruits of Cleavers and Burdocks are very efficient dispersal devices. Human beings eat many fruits and throw away the seeds, often very far indeed from the parents. Vehicles can also disperse seeds. Pineappleweed (*Matricaria discoidea*) seeds have a ribbed surface which helps them cling to muddy car tyres.

Spindle - pink fruit with orange aril

Woody Nightshade - berries, green to orange to yellow to red

Wayfaring Tree - drupes, red to black

PLATE 41: FRUIT AND SEED DISPERSAL BY FORCIBLE EJECTION

Seeds or fruits are sometimes forcibly ejected from the parent plant. This may result from the fruit's own movement. Usually, the drying of the fruit wall sets up tensions which eventually lead to a sudden splitting open in a way that throws out the seeds. In Meadow Cranesbill (*Geranium pratense*) the fruit breaks up into segments and each comes away on the end of a long strip of the style as the structure dries and then curls up and breaks away from the style centre with such force that the fruit segment is shot about 7 feet away, along with the detached strip. In some members of the Pea family (*Fabaceae*), the two walls of the fruit become twisted and eventually split, throwing out the seeds, as shown in Birdsfoot Trefoil (*Lotus corniculatus*). This also happens in some of the Cress family (*Brassicaceae*), such as Hairy Bittercress (*Cardamine hirsuta*), which has fruits that split into two halves which curl upwards rapidly and shoot the seeds out. In violets, the capsule splits longitudinally into three parts, throwing out the seeds as it does so.

Other fruits can split open forcibly because of pressure from the water they contain. The fruits of Indian Balsam (*Impatiens glandulifera*), for instance, become turgid to a point when any slight disturbance can cause them to open violently and contort into a spiral form, throwing out the seeds as they do so.

Meadow Cranesbill - schizocarp before and after breakup

Hairy Bittercress - curling up explosively

Birdsfoot Trefoil - pod (legume) twisted and split

Common Dog Violet - capsule cut open, split in 3

Indian Balsam - capsule before exploding

capsule after exploding

PLATE 42: VEGETATIVE REPRODUCTION

There is a range of devices by which plants reproduce without any sexual processes. Fragments may root as in Slender Speedwell (*Veronica filiformis*) on lawns. Others have bulbils, which are buds stored with food, which can be in the inflorescence, as in Crow Garlic (*Allium vineale*) or on the stem, as in the rare Coralroot (*Cardamine bulbifera)*. These eventually separate from the parent plant and grow into new ones.

Sweet Violet (*Viola odorata*) has branches running along the surface of the ground called runners or stolons. They have small leaves at intervals, each with a bud in its axil which puts down roots and sends up a stem to form a new plant.

Some stems, called rhizomes, are underground, looking more like roots, though they are often distinguished from them by having leaves or buds. They occur in Greater Pond Sedge (*Carex riparia*) and many grasses. *Iris pseudacorus* has a thick rhizome shown in Plate 24. Enchanter's Nightshade (*Circaea lutetiana*) has thin rhizomes. In some plants, such as potato, particular parts of the underground stem become swollen and are called tubers, each of which can produce a new plant. The tuber of Cuckoo Pint (*Arum maculatum*) was shown in Plate 24. The habit of Brambles of burying the end of a normal stem in the ground and putting down roots to form a new plant has been shown in Plate 27.

A swollen stem base is known as a corm, as shown in the misleadingly named Bulbous Buttercup (*Ranunculus bulbosus*) in Plate 24. New plants can sometimes arise from a corm's axillary buds. In Montbretia (*Crocosmia x crocosmioflora*), these produce stolons which can grow up to 30cm long and form new plants at their tips. The corms are unusual in forming vertical chains with contractile roots which drag them deeper into the ground. The chains are fragile and easily separated, making the plant often invasive.

A bulb is also at the foot of the stem, but is really a whole shoot base with the food stored mainly in the fleshy leaf bases, as in cultivated Onion in Plate 24. Buds between the storage leaf bases develop into new plants when favourable conditions return, as shown in Snowdrop (*Galanthis nivalis*). The expansion of a number of close-together Snowdrop bulbs pushes some of them to the surface, where they are blown or carried away and may set down roots elsewhere. New bulbs can also be produced on the sides, as in Crow Garlic (*Allium vineale*).

Vegetative reproduction can also result from production of new shoots from root systems. Roots may also swell with stored food to create root tubers as in Lesser Celandine (*Ficaria verna*) and these can give rise to new plants. Dogwood (*Cornus sanguinea*) sends up suckers from roots, often at a considerable distance from the parent, forming a dense thicket which is eventually suppressed by growth of the strongest saplings.

Crow Garlic - inflorescence of bulbils

Coralroot - stem bulbils

Sweet Violet- stolons

Greater Pond Sedge - rhizome

Montbretia - corms and stolons close-up

Snowdrop - bulb multiplication

Crow Garlic - new bulbs on side

Lesser Celandine - root tubers

Dogwood - thicket of suckers

PLATE 43: ADAPTATION IN GARDEN BORDERS AND ARABLE FIELDS

The study of how plants are able to survive or thrive and interact in the environments they occupy is called ecology. A particular type of environment, such as woodland or grassland, is called a habitat. In each habitat, the plants that grow there have features which enable them to survive. They are said to be adapted to that habitat, and the features are called adaptations. In the plates that follow, the emphasis is on adaptations which can be observed and/or shown by photos, rather than less obvious ones like chemical or physical properties.

The adaptations of plants which invade gardens are mainly concerned with survival under garden management regimes, including such activities as digging and weeding. We can divide these plants into two types - annuals that grow and produce seed early and quickly, and perennials that survive from year to year.

Hairy Bittercress (*Cardamine hirsuta*) is a common early annual in gardens. Gardening is a fairly low-key activity until late April or early May, so any weed that can grow, flower, and seed before then has a distinct advantage. This plant germinates in autumn to be ready for a quick start in spring. The patches of bare soil produced by gardeners help this by removing competitors. Its winter rosettes of leaves can, once spring arrives, quickly reach maturity and disperse seeds, sometimes when barely an inch high. An average plant can produce 600 seeds, which enables it to spread quickly over a substantial area, helped by explosive opening of the fruit as shown in Plate 41, which sends them in different directions and tiny and light seeds which can remain in the air for some distance. Further, the seeds are sticky when moist, so can adhere to shoes, tools and the feet of birds and thus be dispersed to other gardens. Many of the seeds remain dormant and can germinate immediately hoeing brings then to the surface. Another successful early invader is Ivy-leaved Speedwell (*Veronica hederifolia*), which grows prostrate and therefore quickly, since it does not need to develop a supportive stem.

A perennial garden weed is Ground Elder (*Aegopodium podagraria*). It defeats attempts at control by underground rhizomes, which can cover almost a square metre in a single season and remain alive through the winter. Fragments left in the soil can produce new plants. Some plants survive by looking inconspicuous, such as Wood Avens (*Geum urbanum*), which hides among larger plants. Others climb up garden plants, like Greater Bindweed (*Calystegia sepium*).

Arable field borders have some similar features. The land is ploughed to remove competitors and the crop sowed. It is then sprayed with fertilizers and selective weedkillers, but often an unsprayed strip is left at the edges. Ploughed fields not sown with crops for a while also offer good opportunities. Charlock (*Sinapis arvensis*) is a very successful annual arable weed in such conditions. An average plant produces 1-4,000 seeds early in the year because the flowers can pollinate themselves in a closed condition, so don't have to depend on insects or wind or dry weather to reproduce. Seeds are very light, so are easily blown some distance and they can germinate after lying dormant in the soil for many years, so are usually available to colonise wherever an opportunity occurs.

Hairy Bittercress - flowering from winter rosette

colony

Ivy-leaved Speedwell - prostrate growth

Ground Elder - garden weed

Wood Avens - hiding

Greater Bindweed - climbing

Charlock - plant

colony on disturbed ground

large invasion

PLATE 44: ADAPTATION IN GRASSLAND AND LAWNS

The most obvious adaptations of plants growing in grassland and lawns relate to grazing, mowing and cutting. If none of these occur, the vegetation grows to a high level and this is best dealt with by growing tall, like Ragwort (*Senecio jacobaea*) and Cow Parsley (*Anthriscus sylvestris*), which grow vigorously to a height of 2-3 feet. Where grazing or mowing prevent tall growth, plants cope better if their leaves lie flat on the ground, such as those of Dandelion in Plate 5 and Daisy in Plate 4. Some plants in lawns, such as Black Medick (*Medicago lupulina*), have prostrate stems, so that the whole plant is below the mower blades. Spines or prickles can defend plants against grazing damage, as in Stemless Thistle in Plate 1. Others discourage grazing by poisons in their tissues, such as Ragwort and some plants of Birdsfoot Trefoil (*Lotus corniculatus*). Ability to regenerate from ground level helps survival in the presence of grazing, cutting or mowing - Ragwort can produce new shoots on the root, or even root fragments. Slender Speedwell (*Veronica filiformis*), another prostrate species, makes positive use of mowing, in that small bits cut off can root and grow into new plants. A close mat of vegetation makes it difficult for many plants to germinate, which can be circumvented by having seeds which lie dormant for many years and spring up when bare patches appear, as from trampling by stock. Yellow-wort (*Blackstonia perfoliata*) does this.

In the drier grasslands, such as many on chalk or limestone, deep roots can draw water where it collects well below the soil surface, as in Birdsfoot Trefoil (*Lotus corniculatus*). Some plants have devices for conserving the water they have such as Mouse-ear Hawkweed (*Pilosella officinarum*), which has long hairs to trap water vapor on the leaf surfaces and prevent it from escaping into the air.

Ragwort - plant

colony

Cow Parsley - colony

Black Medick - prostrate in lawn

Birdsfoot Trefoil

Slender Speedwell

Yellow-wort

Mouse-ear Hawkweed - leaves with long hairs

PLATE 45: ADAPTATION IN WOODS AND HEDGEROWS

In woods the foliage of the tallest trees is called the canopy. Below them are smaller trees which form an understorey, particularly at the woodland margins, then there is a shrub layer and then a ground flora of mainly herbaceous plants. The sheltered environment provides protection from wind and temperature extremes, and there are ample nutriments from decay of leaf litter and a good supply of water. However, there are problems from lack of light and competition from larger or more vigorous plants. Hedges are rather like miniature woodland, but less shaded and usually more managed. The survival issues are the same.

The most successful canopy trees are likely to be those which grow quickly and become very tall, such as Ash (*Fraxinus excelsior*), which can grow up to almost 100ft. Trees in hedges also do well if they grow fast, such as Hawthorn (*Crataegus monogyna*). All plants below the canopy or within the hedge need to be able to cope with the poor light. Field Maple (*Acer campestre*) seeds under the existing vegetation and grows rapidly to get established before other trees overtake. It conserves its energy by producing only a few flowers or fruits when shade reduces photosynthesis and chances of competing, but reproducing more freely at wood edges or in clearings, where more light is available.

Ash

Hawthorn - in hedgerow

Field Maple

Shrub and ground layer plants often show features which help them cope with poor light. Wood Anemone (*Anemone nemorosa*) is a perennial ground flora plant which does most of its growing and food-making early in the season before the leaves on the trees have fully opened out to shade it. Then the leaves die down and disappear, and it spreads underground by rhizomes, colonising a wide area. Spurge Laurel (*Daphne laureola*) is a shrub, and has large evergreen leaves which allow it to photosynthesise all year and thus make maximum use of woodland light. Yellow Archangel (*Lamiastrum galeobdolon*) is a perennial which produces new leaves in autumn so that they can make food throughout the winter whenever conditions allow. Traveller's Joy (*Clematis vitalba*) eliminates the low light problem by climbing over the woody plants of the hedge holding on by the leaf stalks. A few plants avoid the issue by a saprophytic habit, as in Birdsnest Orchid in Plate 26, or as parasites, such as Toothwort (*Lathraea squamaria*) on Hazel roots, which has no chlorophyll, so is not green.

Wood Anemone

colony in hedgerow

Toothwort - no green

Spurge Laurel

Yellow Archangel - hedgerow group

Traveller's Joy - in hedgerow

holding on by petiole

PLATE 46: ADAPTATION ON WALLS, ROCKS, SAND AND SHINGLE

Walls, rocks, sand and shingle are environments low in nutrients and water and very exposed to dehydration, low temperatures or wind. Attachment of roots is also a problem. Plants in these situations often stay close to the ground, so are less exposed. On rocks, the roots will often penetrate crevices. The mountain plant Moss Campion (*Silene acaulis*), for instance, grows in the form of a mat, which makes it less likely that the roots it forms will be torn off the rock by the force of the wind, reduces evaporation of water and is a defence against frost. Similarly, Sea Sandwort (*Honkenya peploides*), which grows on sandy beaches and the lower part of dunes, is close to the ground, while Biting Stonecrop (*Sedum acre*) forms low mats on walls and other stony or sandy surfaces.

Water retention is also facilitated by more specific devices than mat formation. Many plants in these situations have thick fleshy leaves full of stored water. Sea Sandwort and Biting Stonecrop are examples; while English Stonecrop (*Sedum anglicum*) behaves similarly on seaside cliffs and Yellow-horned Poppy (*Glaucium flavum*) is a seaside shingle plant which has somewhat fleshy leaves. More upright plants often have woolly coverings of hairs which trap water vapour and slow down evaporation, as can be seen in Kidney Vetch (*Anthyllis vulneraria*) on rocks and Sea Stock (*Matthiola sinuata*) on dunes. Rock Samphire (*Crithmum maritimum*) is found on rocks inundated by salt spray, and illustrates the tendency for plant in this situation to have fleshy leaves even though not particularly short of water. It may well be associated with physiological adaptations to cope with large amounts of salt.

Ivy-leaved Toadflax (*Cymbalaria muralis*) shows an adaptation to facilitate establishment of seedlings on hard surfaces. Though the flower stands erect on its stalk to attract insects, the stalks of the ripe fruits bend away from the light so that the seeds are shed towards the mortar joints of the wall, where they take root in the small amounts of soil on the base of the joint.

Moss Campion - low mat on mountain rock

Sea Sandwort - low-growing on sand with thick fleshy leaves

Biting Stonecrop - wall, prostrate

English Stonecrop - fleshy leaves

Yellow-horned poppy - upright on shingle with fleshy leaves

Kidney Vetch - dense woolly hairs

Sea Stock - woolly hairs

Rock Samphire - on stones with fleshy leaves

Ivy-leaved Toadflax - on mortared wall

fruit stalks bent towards wall

PLATE 47: ADAPTATION IN WET PLACES

There is a variety of habitats in wet places - ponds, rivers, streams, canals, and bogs, marshes and ditches where the plants are basically growing in soil but it's more or less permanently waterlogged. Not only is water readily available for the plant's life processes, but it also provides support, so it is uneconomic in still or slow-moving water to have strong or large roots or strong stems and leaves, and many plants adapt by dispensing with them. Leaves do, however, have to either resist or otherwise minimize the risk of damage from water currents. There need to be ways of getting oxygen to the underground parts, since absorption from water is less efficient than from the air. Buoyancy may be needed for some parts of the plant. There are opportunities for making use of water movements for pollination and seed dispersal and for storing food and surviving winters underwater. These adaptations are illustrated here.

Stream Water Crowfoot (*Ranunculus penicillatus*) is found in running water. It has all its leaves submerged and divided into narrow segments, so that the current easily flows past them and doesn't sweep them away. It anchors in the mud below by adventitious roots at the stem nodes.

White Waterlily (*Nymphaea alba*) is a perennial plant with a stout rhizome rooted in soil at the bottom of the water. Its leaves are large and floating so that they do not sink easily, and they are strong and leathery, which reduces the likelihood of damage from water currents. They have a waxy upper surface so that water rolls off in drops instead of forming pools which would interfere with taking in oxygen and carbon dioxide from the air. The leaf and flower stalks have no underwater leaves on them so that the water can easily flow past without damage, and there are air spaces and passages in the leaves and stems, so that air can get quickly and easily from the air to the underwater parts. The flower is protected from submergence by its position among the large floating leaves. After fertilisation it sinks and forms a large spherical berry. When ripe it splits to release a mass of seeds which rises to the surface. Each seed is covered with a mass of spongy tissue (aril), whose air bubbles keep it afloat for dispersal. These gradually disappear and the seed sinks to the bottom, where it germinates.

Marsh Marigold (*Caltha palustris*) has hollow stems which enable oxygen and carbon dioxide to get to the underwater parts. The carpel often has air spaces which are likely to enable wider dispersal by wind or water. The plant has an additional adaptation in that, if it gets submerged, it produces tiny leaves on long petioles, presenting less resistance to water flow.

Great Hairy Willowherb (*Epilobium hirsutum*) is a plant of damp habitats such as ditches and by watersides, which produces tall thick colonies which crowd out competitors. It spreads by long horizontal stems, which are either rhizomes in the basal mud or stolons in the water and have air spaces, so that oxygen and carbon dioxide can move easily between the different parts.

Stream Water Crowfoot - long narrow leaf divisions

White Waterlily - plant

White Waterlily - long petioles

air spaces in petiole

Marsh Marigold - view

hollow stem

plant

Great Hairy Willowherb - colony

stolon

PLATE 48: ENGLISH NAMES FOR FLOWERING PLANTS

English names are also referred to as popular names and vernacular names. However, most came from early physicians and herbalists, while many others have been invented by botanists ancient and modern. For the earliest name, the derivation is mostly not known - Gentian, for instance, is simply the name given by the Roman naturalist Pliny. Name derivations which are known or can be intelligently guessed come mainly from characteristics or uses of plants.

Many English names refer to overall appearance, such as Golden Rod. Others come from specific characteristics, such as the flower shape in Bee Orchid (Plates 12 and 30), the flower arrangement in Clustered Bellflower and Town Hall Clock (Plate 11), and the shape of the fruits in Common Pennycress. Bittersweet (Plate 40) is named after the initial sweet taste of the berries which quickly becomes bitter, while Stinkweed and Fragrant Orchid are named after their smell.

The habits of plants can be indicated by names. This may include where it grows - as in Waterlily and Water Crowfoot (both shown in Plate 47). Methods of growth can give rise to names, as in Hop (from a Saxon word meaning climb) and Greater Bindweed (Plates 22 and 43). Time of flowering leads to such names as Evening Primrose, while Buddleia has been called Butterfly Bush because it is so attractive to them.

The uses of plants are another source of names. Cress is from an Old English word meaning eat. Butcher's Broom was once used for sweeping butchers' floors. Medical uses have spawned many names. Self-heal was a dressing for wounds. Stitchwort (Plate 32) was for a pain in the side, while Feverfew explains itself. Some indicate that the plant is useless or harmful. Thus Cow Parsley (Plates 16 and 44) is fit only for cows and Fool's Parsley poisonous.

Some plants are named after gods or holy people, perhaps because they were involved in religious ceremonies. Carline Thistle is named after the King Charlemagne - it was supposedly divinely revealed to him as a remedy against the plague - and it does have some resemblance to a crown before it opens.

The use of English names is variable. An attempt to systematise them was made in *English Names of Wild Flowers* by Perring, Dony and Jury, published by the *Botanical Society of the British Isles* in 1974 and revised in 1986. It has been largely accepted by the professional botanical world. However, not everyone agrees. In this guide, their recommended uses of hyphens in spellings which defeat normal memory are avoided. Most names are written either as separate words without hyphens (e.g. Dog Rose) or as words joined into a longer word (e.g. Rockrose). All the main words have capitals. There should be no difficulty in identifying a plant as the same with different spellings.

Golden Rod

Clustered Bellflower

Common Pennycress

Evening Primrose

Fragrant Orchid

Butterfly Bush

Fool's Parsley

Hop

Butcher's Broom

Feverfew

Carline Thistle

PLATE 49: NAMING AND CLASSIFYING FLOWERING PLANTS

To give a plant an English name is to classify it - we are saying that it belongs to the collection (or class) of somewhat differing plants which bear that name. However, it is often not botanically correct. Marsh Marigold, for instance, is not botanically a marigold. For correct classification, we use botanical names.

In botanical classification, some groups of plants with very similar structure are regarded as forming a species, which will have a scientific name and an English name. For instance, Bulbous Buttercup is the species *Ranunculus bulbosus*. Species considered to be related because of common evolutionary origin are grouped together to form a genus (plural genera). Thus all the different species of buttercup - Creeping Buttercup, Acrid Buttercup and so on belong to the genus *Ranunculus*. In turn related genera are grouped together in families, so that buttercups and their relatives all belong to the family *Ranunculaceae*. Closely related families are grouped together into orders, so that the *Ranunculacea*e are included in the Order *Ranunculales*, which also includes the Poppy and Berberis families. Orders are grouped into higher level groupings. From a number of schemes proposed, one of the most widely accepted has three groups called Pre-dicots, Monocots and Eudicots, distinguished by microscopic characters and therefore not defined here, and these make up the class *Angiospermae* (the flowering plants). Other classes incorporate mosses and liverworts, ferns and their relatives and conifers, and the whole collection makes up the Plant Kingdom. Fungi, Algae, Lichens and Bacteria, treated as classes within the Plant Kingdom till at least the 1960s, are now regarded as members of different kingdoms. All names, whether species, genera etc, are referred to generally as taxa (singular taxon) and this area of study is known as taxonomy.

A complication is that some species are divided into subspecies, and they and the species themselves are sometimes divided into varieties. Further, there is often no way of saying exactly how to determine where the boundaries between different species lie and exactly what species belong to one genus rather than another - so different schemes and names will be encountered. To avoid feelings of inadequacy, it is necessary to understand that no one has ever come up with a satisfactory definition of the term "species". The most common attempts have centred on the fact that most species do not hybridise with other species to produce fertile offspring. However different species of violets and some orchids manage this, and are examples of this rule not working, while some plants in the same species cannot carry our sexual reproduction at all, relying on vegetative methods

Taxonomic categories and relationships

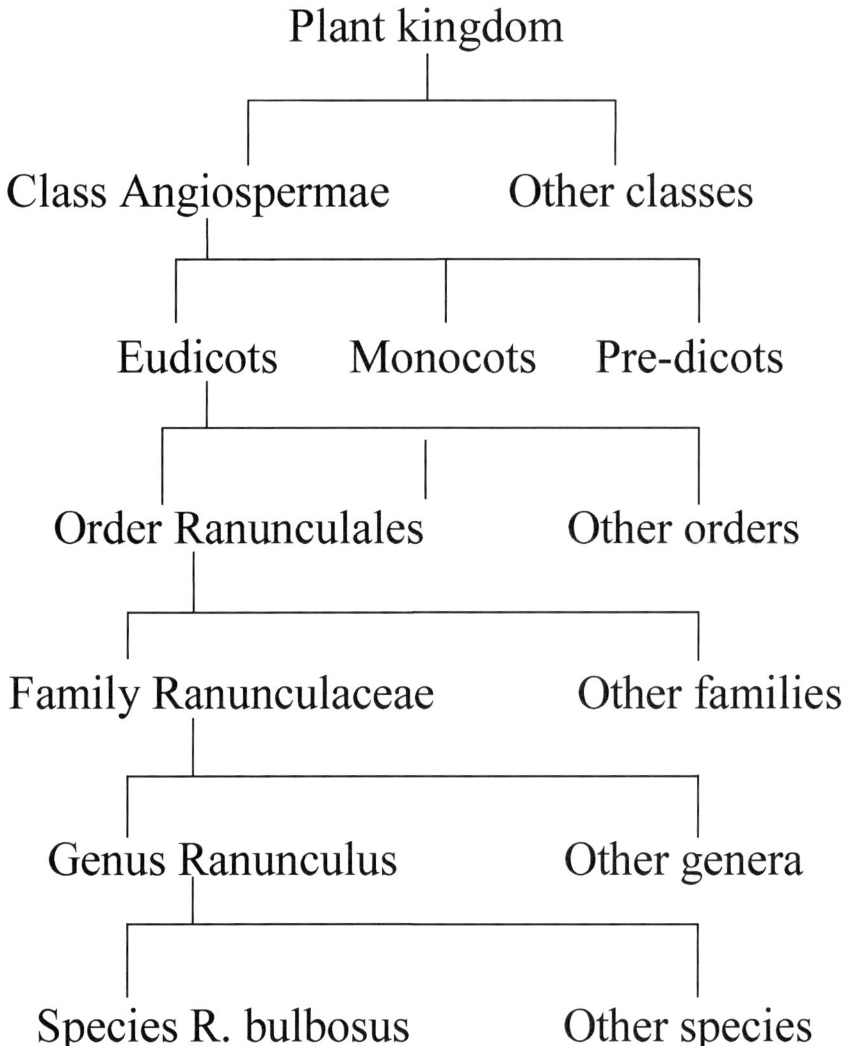

PLATE 50: THE BUTTERCUP FAMILY AS AN EXAMPLE OF CLASSIFICATION

The *Ranunculaceae* (Buttercup family) illustrates the classification in Plate 49. Like most families, it is defined mainly by flower structure, with vegetative characters becoming more important at the species level. The flowers are mainly radially symmetrical and hypogynous i.e. the sepals, petals and stamens are inserted below the ovary. These parts are free rather than fused. Most typically, the genus *Ranunculus* (buttercups) has 5 sepals, mostly 5 petals and a large number of stamens and carpels, and each carpel has one ovule. Each petal has a nectary at the base (Plate 14). The fruit is a collection of achenes (Plate 17).

Other genera show variations from this pattern. Some have no differentiation between petals and sepals, the single whorl usually being interpreted as sepals. This is petal-like in *Caltha* (Plate 8), where it is yellow, and *Anemone,* where it is white in *A. nemorosa*, (Plate 31) but green like sepals in *Helleborus* (Plate 8). The number of sepals is 5-20 in *Anemone* and 5-10 in *Caltha*. *Helleborus* has 5-12 petals which are green and look like and function as tubular nectaries (Plate 14). *Ficaria* (Plate 11) has 3 sepals and 7-12 petals. *Clematis* usually has 4 sepals, which are like petals. *Aquilegia* (Plate 14) has both sepals and petals, which both look like petals. There is a smaller number of carpels in *Helleborus* (3-10), *Caltha* (5-15) and *Aquilegia* (5-10), and each has numerous ovules. *Caltha* (Plates 18 and 36), *Aquilegia* and *Helleborus* have follicles instead of achenes. Old Man's Beard (*Clematis vitalba*) has a feathery elongated style on each achene (Plate 37). *Aquilegia* has its nectaries in a long hollow spur at the bottom of each of the five petals. *Aconitum* (Monkshood) has the upper sepal forming a hood over the rest of the flower, making it bilaterally symmetrical. *Thalictrum* (Meadow Rue) has stamens more conspicuous than the other parts. *Clematis* species are woody climbers (Plate 45).

Though distinctions between species are of smaller degree than those between genera, *Ranunculus* has some striking differences. The common buttercups *R. bulbous* (Bulbous Buttercup), *R. acris* (Meadow Buttercup) and *R. repens* (Creeping Buttercup) all have yellow petals, along with about 10 other species in Britain, whereas the species called Water Crowfoot have white flowers, sometimes with a yellow patch at the base of each petal. *R. bulbosus* has its sepals strongly reflexed (bent downwards against the flower stalk as in Plate 9), while the other two common yellow species have them growing out sideways (patent). *R. repens* is distinguished from the other two by its prostrate main stems rooting at the nodes, and *R. bulbosus* by the corm at the base of the stem (Plate 24). The Water Crowfoot species are to a large extent distinguished by whether they have aquatic leaves with branching thread-like segments or floating flat leaves or both (as in Plate 47). Thus *R. aquatilis* (Common Water Crowfoot) can have either or both, whereas *R. fluitans* (River Water Crowfoot) has aquatic leaves only and these are very long with parallel segments.

***Helleborus foetidus* -**
floral parts from above

vertical section

***Aconitum napellus* -**
zygomorphic, hood

***Clematis vitalba* - 4 petals**

***Thalictrum flavum* - conspicuous stamens**

***Ranunculus acris* - sepals patent**

***Ranunculus repens* - runners**

***Ranunculus aquaticus* -**
floating and submerged leaves

***Ranunculus fluitans* -**
long submerged leaves

PLATE 51: BOTANICAL AND HORTICULTURAL NAMES

Botanical names, also referred to as scientific names, Latin names and binomial names, derive from the classification system in Plates 49 and 50. They use the binomial system - each name of two separate words - the generic name (i.e. the name of the genus) first and the specific name (i.e. the name of the species) second. The generic name has an initial capital letter, but the specific name does not. Thus, Bulbous Buttercup is *Ranunculus bulbosus*. Specific names are sometimes made up of two or more words joined by hyphens e.g. Bluebell is *Hyacinthoides non-scripta*. Each species name is followed by the name (usually abbreviated) of the first person to assign it. Many simply have "L.", which stands for Linnaeus, the originator of modern botanical nomenclature - hence *Ranunculus bulbosus* L. After a first use of the generic name in a written document, it is often abbreviated to the initial capital letter with a full stop after it e.g. *R. bulbosus* for *Ranunculus bulbosus*. A specific name has to agree grammatically with the generic name, that is, both have to have masculine, feminine or neuter endings. This often means the ending is the same, as in *Ranunculus bulbosus*, where both are masculine. However, because of the many different Latin and Greek endings used, the grammatical agreement is often not evident, as in Hawthorn (*Crataegus monogyna*). We do not know for certain how Greeks and Romans pronounced their words, so pronunciation varies, even between experts. Pronunciation rules have been offered by various authors, but they are too complicated for normal use.

Hybrids are named in two ways, with both often quoted. One has the names of the two parent species with an x between them, as in *Hyacinthoides non-scripta x Hyacinthoides hispanica* for the hybrid between Bluebell and Spanish Bluebell. The other is the generic name followed by a name for the hybrid itself - *Hyacinthoides x massartiana*. Variants and hybrids of species developed in cultivation are referred to as cultivars and clones. A cultivar is bred, whereas a clone is propagated vegetatively, e.g. by cuttings, layering, budding, root division, grafts, etc. Both are usually given cultivar names. These begin with a capital letter and are enclosed in single quotes e.g. the variant of Meadow Cranesbill called *Geranium pratense* 'Splishsplash'.

A family's name is formed from the name of one of its genera by replacing its ending with *-aceae* - thus *Ranunculus* becomes *Ranunculaceae*. Some long-established alternatives names are also used, e.g. *Compositae* (the Daisy family).

A botanical name is intended to give a single label to be used and understood by all long-term. However, since they are based on evolutionary relationships, increases in knowledge and different opinions lead to not infrequent variations. The same genus can even be in different families in different books.

Botanical names come mostly from Latin, but some from Greek. Thus, the quick-growing *Salix caprea* (Goat Willow) comes from the Latin salio, meaning to spring out, and caprea meaning she-goat, because the leaves are relished by goats. In *Aethusa cynapium* (Fool's parsley) (Plate 48), the generic name is from the Greek aithos, meaning fire (from the burning taste), while the specific name is from the Greek kyon, meaning dog and and apium meaning parsley, i.e. it's a parsley fit only for dogs. For large numbers of names, however, we know only that they were used by Greek or Roman authorities. Names from other languages can be latinised - as in Fumaria (Fumitory), from the French "fume de terre", meaning smoke of the earth. Plants can also be named after famous botanists, such as *Sherardia arvensis* (Field Madder), after the 17th to 18th Century English botanist James Sherard.

Specific names frequently refer to physical features or habits of plant, such as *Cirsium acaule* (Dwarf Thistle - no stem, Plate 1). The growth form is also used, as in *Ranunculus repens* (Creeping Buttercup - Plate 50). Life cycles are referred to in *Adonis annua* (Pheasant's Eye) and *Bellis perennis* (Daisy). Quite a few names refer to habitat, though the words used sometimes don't indicate the habitat occupied today - *Fagus sylvatica* (Beech - woodland), *Vicia sativa* (Common Vetch - cultivated).

Hyacinthoides x massartiana =
Hyacinthoides non-scripta x Hyacinthoides hispanica

Hyacinthoides non-scripta

Hyacinthoides hispanica

***Geranium pratense* 'Splishsplash'**

Fumitory (*Fumaria officinalis*) - from French 'fume-de-terre'

PLATE 52: BEGINNING TO IDENTIFY FLOWERING PLANTS

The perfect guide for enabling beginners to identify flowering plants is *The Collins Pocket Guide to Wild Flowers* by McClintock and Fitter, which has illustrations arranged by the colour of the flowers, with flowers of similar structure grouped together within each colour section, and a brief but useful description of each plant. It is out-of-print, but it is easy to find second-hand at give-away prices. Alternatively, the beginner can make use of one of the excellent guides which arrange illustrations by family. New ones regularly appear, so recommendations are soon likely to be out of date, but some current examples to consider, all copiously illustrated, are:

- *Wild Flowers of Britain and Ireland.* Marjorie Blamey and Richard and Alastair Fitter, which is very comprehensive and has some similar species grouped together.
- *Complete British Wild Flowers* by Paul Sterry, which omits trees and difficult species, but has good descriptions and diagnostic features.
- *Philip's Guide to Wild Flowers of Britain and North Europe* by Bob Gibbons and Peter Brough.
- *Collins British Wild Flower Guide* by David Streeter and others.

Identification guides for specific groups of plants and the flowering plants of particular geographical areas are also available.

Though it is possible to just look through the illustrations in these books to find one that looks like the plant to be identified, the process is facilitated by an ability to identify its family. Only some authors offer guidance here. The descriptions and illustrations on the next few pages give key features of some of the larger and most easily described families, which allow assignation to a family of the most characteristic plants. Sometimes, it may be necessary to search within two or more families, particularly as different books may put the same plant in different families.

Papaveraceae (Poppy family) - 2 free sepals, 4 free petals, numerous free stamens and carpels joined into a single ovary e.g. Long-headed poppy (*Papaver dubium*).
Ranunculaceae (Buttercup family) - free petals and/or sepals and numerous stamens, all inserted below the numerous carpels e.g. Creeping Buttercup. (*Ranunculus repens*) and *R. acris* in Plate 50.
Saxifragaceae - 5 each of sepals and petals, 10 stamens, 2 carpels partly or completely joined e.g. Starry Saxifrage (*Saxifraga stellaris*).
Crassulaceae - 5 each of sepals and petals, 10 free stamens, 2 carpels partly or completely joined, leaves often succulent e.g. White Stonecrop (*Sedum album*).
Fabaceae (Pea family) - 2 wing-like petals, a large upright petal and 2 others fused into a keel protecting the sexual parts, a tube of 10 stamens and a single ovary and style e.g. Restharrow (*Ononis repens*).
Rosaceae (Rose family) - 5 each of free sepals and petals, numerous free stamens often inserted on top or around the free or fused carpels e.g. Dog Rose

(*Rosa canina*).
Euphorbiaceae (Spurge family) - no petals and sepals, inflorescence a cup containing a roundish ovary, 2-5 glands and 5 tiny stamens e.g. Balkan Spurge (*Euphorbia oblongata*).

Papaveraceae
Long-headed poppy

Ranunculaceae
Creeping Buttercup

Saxifragaceae
Starry Saxifrage

Crassulaceae
White Stonecrop

Fabaceae
Restharrow

Rosaceae
Dog Rose

Euphorbiaceae
Balkan Spurge

PLATE 52 (continued)

Hypericaceae - 5 each of free sepals and petals, stamens many, in 3 or 5 bundles, single ovary with 3 or 5 styles, often glands on flowers and leaves (Plates 5, 9 and 11) e.g. Tall Tutsan (*Hypericum x inodorum*).
Geraniaceae (Cranesbill family) - 5 sepals, 5 petals and 5 or 10 stamens, all free, and ovary of 5 joined carpels with styles joined into an upright column e.g. Hedgerow Cranesbill (*Geranium pyrenaicum*).
Malvaceae (Mallow family) - 5 sepals, 5 petals and numerous stamens joined only at the base and a single ovary e.g. Dwarf Mallow (*Malva neglecta*).
Onagraceae (Willowherb family) - 4 sepals, 4 petals and 8 stamens, all free and borne on top of a long single ovary e.g. Rosebay Willowherb (*Chamerion angustifolium*) and American Willowherb (*Epilobium ciliatum*).
Brassicaceae (Cabbage or Cress family) - 4 free sepals, 4 free petals looking like a cross, 2, 4 or 6 free stamens and a single ovary and style e.g. Lady's Smock (*Cardamine pratensis*).
Caryophyllaceae (Pink family) - 4-5 each of free or joined sepals and free petals, stamens twice as many as the sepals and a single ovary with 3 or 5 styles e.g. Sea Campion (*Silene maritima*).
Primulaceae (Primrose family) - 5 sepals free or joined, 5 petals in pale colours joined into a tube with the 5 stamens borne on the corolla tube and a single ovary and style e.g. Scarlet Pimpernel (*Anagallis arvensis*).
Rubiaceae (Bedstraw family) - sepals inconspicuous, 4 very tiny petals, 4-5 stamens and leaves in whorls e.g. Heath Bedstraw (*Galium saxatile*).
Boraginaceae (Forget-me-not family) - 5 sepals and petals each joined into a tube, 5 stamens borne on the corolla tube, single ovary, inflorescence spiral e.g. Viper's Bugloss (*Echium vulgare*), Water Forget-me-not (*Myosotis scorpioides*).
Solanaceae (Nightshade family) - 5 sepals and 5 petals each fused into a tube, 5 stamens borne on the corolla tube with anthers sometimes joined into a tube and a single ovary e.g. Bittersweet (*Solanum dulcamara*).
Veronicaceae (Speedwell family), included in *Scrophulariaceae* in some books - petals joined with 4 lobes at the top not all the same size and shape and sometimes with a spur, 2 or 4 stamens and a single ovary and style e.g. Germander Speedwell (*Veronica chamaedrys*), Purple Toadflax (*Linaria purpurea*).

Hypericaceae
Tall Tutsan

Geraniaceae
Hedgerow Cranesbill

Malvaceae
Dwarf Mallow

Onagraceae
Rosebay Willowherb

American Willowherb

Brassicaceae
Lady's Smock

Caryophyllaceae
Sea Campion

Primulaceae
Scarlet Pimpernel

Rubiaceae
Heath Bedstraw

Boraginaceae
Viper's Bugloss

Water Forget-me-not

Solanaceae
Bittersweet

Veronicaceae
Germander Speedwell

Purple Toadflax

PLATE 52 (continued)

Plantaginaceae (Plantain family) - brownish spike-like inflorescence and leaves usually all in a basal rosette e.g. Greater Plantain (*Plantago major*).
Scrophulariaceae (Figwort family) - petals and sepals each fused into a tube with 4-5 lobes, 4 stamens borne on the petals and a single ovary e.g. Twiggy Mullein (*Verbascum virgatum*).
Lamiaceae (Deadnettle family) - both sepals and petals joined into a tube which divides at the top into an upper and a lower lip, 4 stamens, stems square in cross-section e.g. Common Hempnettle (*Galeopsis tetrahit*).
Campanulaceae (Bellflower family) - 5 sepals and 5 petals, each fused into a tube with 5 lobes at the top, 5 stamens and a single ovary with 3 or 5 styles e.g. Adria Bellflower (*Campanula portenschlagiana*).
Asteraceae (Daisy family) - "flowers" in heads composed of ray florets, disc florets or both e.g. Sneezewort (*Achillea ptarmica*), Beaked Hawksbeard (*Crepis vesicaria*), Wormwood (*Artemisia absinthum*).
Dipsacaceae (Teasel family) - many small flowers in heads, flowers tubular and unequally lobed at top e.g. Field Scabious (*Knautia arvensis*).
Apiaceae (Parsley family) - inflorescence an umbel and flowers with 5 free petals and 5 free stamens and a single ovary with two styles e.g. Corky-fruited Water Dropwort (*Oenanthe pimpinelloides*).
Liliaceae (Lily family) (with *Alliaceae and Asparagaceae*, sometimes included in it) - 6 free tepals, all alike, 6 stamens and a single ovary, commonly with 3 lobes e.g. Spring Squill (*Scilla verna*).
Orchidaceae (Orchid family) - 6 free tepals forming 2 lips, pollinia instead of stamens e.g. Common Spotted Orchid (*Dactylorhiza fuchsii*).

The well-known Pansy and Violet flowers of *Violaceae* are in Plates 9 and 30. *Ericaceae*, which includes heaths, defeats description, as do *Convolvulaceae*, which includes bindweeds (Plates 11, 23, 28 and 43), the parasitic *Orobranchaceae,* often with no green coloration (Plates 26 and 45) and *Polygonaceae,* which often have fused stipules encircling the stem, as in Knotgrass (*Polygonum arenastrum*). Goosefoots (*Amaranthaceae*) often have a grey mealy inflorescence, as in Fat Hen (*Chenopodium album*).

Plantaginaceae
Greater Plantain

Lamiaceae
Common Hempnettle

Scrophulariaceae
Twiggy Mullein

Asteraceae

Sneezewort

Beaked Hawksbeard

Wormwood

Campanulaceae

Adria Bellflower

Dipsacaceae

Field Scabious

***Apiaceae* Corky-fruited Water Dropwort**

Liliaceae

Spring Squill

***Orchidaceae* Common Spotted Orchid**

Polygonaceae

Knotgrass

Amaranthaceae

Fat Hen

PLATE 53: IDENTIFICATION BEYOND THE BEGINNING STAGE

Eventually, familiarity with botanical names is essential, and most popular books include them. To make effective use of them in identification, botanists use a flora, in which the plants are arranged according to plant classification. Identification is through keys, often aided by line drawings. The standard flora for Britain and Ireland is Clive Stace's large New *Flora of the British Isles*, third edition 2010. The slimmer version of the 2nd edition, *Field Flora of the British Isles*, is more portable, but some names and classification are outdated.

Floras contain mostly two kinds of key. The most common is the dichotomous key, which consists of a series of numbered choices, each requiring the user to choose which of two alternatives applies to the plant under consideration. Each choice either identifies the plant or refers the user to a new numbered choice point. The following is a specially constructed simple key to the commonest species of wild poppy, all in the genus *Papaver*.

1. Leaves bluish green, clasping stem at base *P. somniferum* (Opium Poppy)
1. Leaves normal green, not clasping the stem 2
2. Fruit capsule less than two times as long as wide P. *rhoeas* (Common Poppy)
2. Fruit capsule more than two times as long as wide *P. dubium* (Long-headed poppy)

If your plant is *P. rhoeas*, Choicepoint 1 will identify it as the second option (Leaves normal green, not clasping the stem) and thus direct you to Choicepoint 2. At Choicepoint 2, the capsule less than two times as long as wide will take you to *P. rhoeas*. It is wise to confirm the identification with the description of the species in the flora to ensure that it matches. If it doesn't, go back to the key to see if you might have misinterpreted anything. With any key, of course, there may be other species which are not included and it may be one of those, in which case a more comprehensive key would be needed.

***Papaver somniferum* - leaves bluish**

***Papaver rhoeas* - leaves green**

***Papaver rhoeas* and *dubium* - fruits**

A dichotomous key is often supplemented by a multi-access key, which consists of a list of characteristics, most commonly labelled with letters. The plant is checked against each characteristic and a note made of the letter of each one that applies. The list of letters is checked against the species list in the key to find which species is the closest match. The following is a specially constructed simple key to the commonest species of *Epilobium* (willowherbs).

A. Stigma 4-lobed, sometimes with the lobes pressed close together
B. Stigma club-shaped
C. Stem hairs near apex all flat against stem
D. Stem hairs near apex spreading
E. Spreading hairs 0 or all glandular (i.e. with rounded heads) - see Plate 2
F. Some spreading hairs present and not glandular
G. Petals 10-16mm long
H. Petals 3-10mm long

E. montanum (Broad-leaved Willowherb) ADEH
E. hirsutum (Great Willowherb) ADFG
E. parviflorum (Hoary Willowherb) ADFH
E. tetragonum (Square-stalked Willowherb) BCE
E. ciliatum (American Willowherb) BDEH

Only the letters that clearly apply are used. Thus, for *E. parviflorum*, it is not always easy to see the lobes of the stigma, but the other letters distinguish that species from the others. G and H cannot be used for E. *tetragonum* because plants can have either, but none of the others have the combination BCE.

Epilobium montanum

Epilobium parviflorum

In Stace's flora, the first key leads you to the family. Within each family, there is a key to the genera, and within each genus there is a key to the species. Where a species is divided into subspecies, there will be a key to these. There is a glossary defining the technical terms used. Stace also advises that, if it is difficult to make a decision at a particular choicepoint, you should follow both choices in the rest of the key, when it will often become clear which is correct.

Some families and genera are widely held to be more difficult than others, for instance grasses (*Poaceae*), the Parsley family (*Apiaceae*), and the Mustard or Cress family (*Brassicaceae*). There are publications on them, but it is advisable to join a local botanical or natural history society for hands-on help. The *Botanical Society of Britain and Ireland* is also a helpful resource.

PLATE 54: CONIFERS

The term "Conifer" is commonly used as a popular name for the Gymnosperms. Gymnosperm literally means "naked seed" and refers to the ovules, later seeds, lying on a scale leaf without the enclosing ovary and surrounding sepals and petals found in flowering plants. Like flowering plants, they are vascular plants, i.e. they have specialised tissues for conducting water and food materials around the plant. Only three species are believed to be native to Britain and Ireland, of which Scots Pine (*Pinus sylvestris*) is so only in ancient pine forests, and introduced elsewhere, while Juniper (*Juniperus communis*) is rare.

Almost all conifers in Britain and Ireland are forest trees in origin, though often planted today, and almost all are evergreen. Scot Pine is seen most as an individual tree and often has reddish-tinted bark towards the top. Its branches grow in apparent whorls of three, giving it a symmetrical appearance which is frequently lost by branches falling or dying off in the wind-swept sites in which it is commonly planted. Yew is a rather spreading tree, encountered mainly in churchyards. Juniper is a grey-green evergreen tree or 4-12 feet high shrub. The British Isles also have over 40 species which are introductions, some of which have reproduced themselves and escaped into the wild.

The leaves on most conifers are needle-like but borne in varying arrangements. Yew (*Taxus baccata*) has leaves up to an inch long and in two horizontal rows, dark green and each with two white stripes on the lower side. The leaves of Juniper are in whorls of three on young branches but in opposite pairs when older, and are spine-tipped and awl-shaped, 5-19mm long with a broad whitish band on the upper side. In Scots Pine there are two kinds of leaves, scale leaves on the main stems and twisted linear bluish green leaves in pairs and up to 8cm long on short branches.

Conifer leaves typically have thick, largely waterproof surfaces which reduce water loss in species living in hot, dry conditions and protect against frost in the large number which live in cold situations. Their evergreen nature gives a longer period in which food can be made in cold conditions where photosynthesis is slowed down. The tough fruit coverings of many conifers may also be an adaptation to cold, and so may wind pollination, because of the scarcity of insects to carry out pollination in those circumstances. The longevity of Yew helps make up for the lack of light for photosynthesis even in the dense shade of a beech wood understorey. It is protected against predators by poisons and a scattering of silica, harder than tooth enamel, in the leaves.

Some wild flower identification books include conifers. *British Trees: A photographic guide to every common species* by Paul Sterry (Collins 2008) has been enthusiastically reviewed, and *Trees: A field guide to the Trees of Britain and North Europe* by White, White and Walters looks helpful. The Natural History Museum in London has an interactive on-line identification guide.

Scots Pine - tree in ancient forest

planted elsewhere

leaves in pairs

reddish bark

Yew - tree in churchyard

in woodland understorey

leaves above

leaves below

Juniper - shrub

leaves and male cones

PLATE 55: REPRODUCTION IN CONIFERS

The reproductive structures of conifers are borne on scales called sporophylls and are typically arranged in cones. In Scots Pine, male and female cones are borne on the same tree and are from 3-7cm long at maturity, though more pea-size early on. The young male cones are borne in clusters in the axils of scale leaves near the base of the year's new growth and are yellow at first and sometimes crimson at maturity. Each consists of a number of spirally arranged sporophylls, each with two pollen sacs attached beneath it. The young female cones are borne singly or in groups up to five in the axils of scale leaves at the ends of the new growth. They are globular to conical, and are initially pink, later rosy purple. Each is made up of spirally arranged bracts, each with a sporophyll bearing two ovules above it. When ripe, the pollen sacs split open and pollen is transferred from the male to the female cones by the wind, each pollen grain having two balloon-like air sacs to help keep it in the air as long as possible. The sporophylls of the female cone separate, leaving gaps for the wind to blow the pollen in to the ovules. The ovules then secrete a liquid which absorbs the pollen grains to allow fertilisation. After pollination the sporophylls of the female cone close up to protect the developing seed and gradually become brown and woody. The female cone reaches its third year before producing the mature seed, which has a delicate wing about three times as long as itself to help its dispersal by wind. The cone sporophylls gape to allow their escape in dry weather but close up when it's wet.

The male and female structures of Juniper are usually on different plants. They are in small yellowish cones, the male shown in Plate 54. The sporophylls in the female cone fuse and become succulent after fertilization, so that they look like, first green, then blue-black berries with a bloom, each with 1-6 seeds. Birds are the most important dispersal agents and their digestive processes apparently do not harm most of the seeds and may actually enhance germination.

In Yew male and female structures are normally, but not always, on different trees. The male is a cone but the female body consists instead of a single ovule borne on a scale near the end of a branch. The fruit which develops from the ovule after pollination, which is by wind, is surrounded by a succulent red outgrowth called an aril, which attracts birds to eat it. They usually drop the seed afterwards to disperse it. Squirrels are also known to disperse it by eating the aril and seed, and regurgitating the seed.

Scots Pine - male cones

female cone at 3 stages

Yew - young male cones

mature male cones

young and mature fruit

female reproductive organs

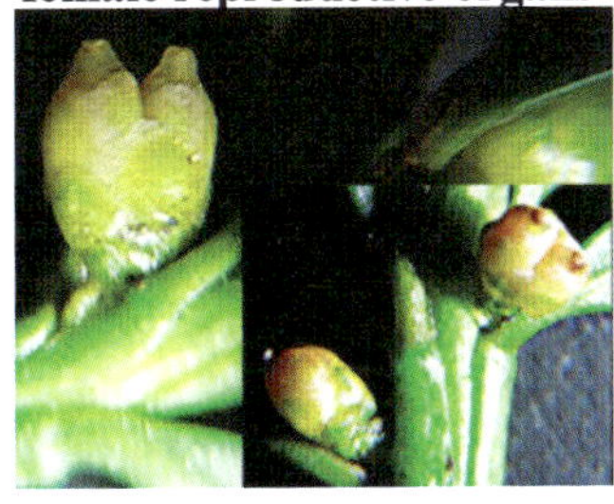

Juniper - female cones

berries

PLATE 56: FERNS AND THEIR ALLIES

Ferns and their allies, like flowering plants and conifers, are vascular plants, but differ in not producing either flowers or seeds. It is not even obvious that they reproduce sexually, since the plant as we normally see it produces only spores by asexual methods. However, when a spore has been dispersed and germinates, it gives rise to a tiny flat structure called a prothallus. This bears even tinier sex organs on the underside. The male organ produces spermatozoids, which are minute single-celled bodies with whip-like threads called flagella which, in wet conditions, propel them through the layer of moisture between the prothallus and the soil to reach and fertilise the female bodies. From this union the normal plant that we see grows, still attached to the prothallus until the latter dies. The adult plant shows a range of forms, some of which are described below.

Ferns and their relatives have been grouped together as the *Pteridophyta* or *Pteropsida.* They include clubmosses, quillworts, adder's tongues and moonworts, which are low, creeping, shortly erect or otherwise inconspicuous plants which are rarely both encountered and attended to by amateur naturalists. The most striking and better known ferns and horsetails, both have a rhizome for the main stem, but horsetails also have aerial stems bearing whorls of short, one-veined leaves forming sheaths at intervals, while the ferns mostly have separate leaves arising at ground level and with more complex vein systems. Species illustrated here are Fir Clubmoss (*Huperzia selago*), Moonwort (*Botrychium lunaria*), Quillwort (*Isoetes histrix*), Adder's Tongue (*Ophioglossum vulgatum*), Giant Horsetail (*Equisetum telmateia*) and Bracken (*Pteridium aquilinum*).

Some wild flower identification books include these groups. For ferns specifically, *The Fern Guide* 3rd edition by James Merryweather (Field Studies Council 2007) has been well reviewed, as has his easily portable *Key to Common Ferns* and his DVD *British Ferns.* Francis Rose's excellent 1989 *Colour Identification Guide to the Grasses, Sedges, Rushes and Ferns of the British Isles and North Western Europe* is still available.

Fir Clubmoss **Quillwort** **Adder's Tongue**

Moonwort - young

mature

Giant Horsetail - many stems from rhizome

stem with whorls of branches

Bracken - woodland colony

frond from underground rhizome

PLATE 57: HORSETAILS

The basic horsetail structure is best seen in one of the rarer ones - the Giant Horsetail (*Equisetum telmateia*), which is typical enough to show what the group is like. As seen in Plate 56, many stems come up from a rhizome and bear whorls of short, one-veined, tooth-like leaves at regular intervals which are combined into sheaths at their bases. The number of teeth at each sheath is the same as the number of ridges on the stem. Dense whorls of branches spring from the area of each sheath. The stem is white, whereas in other horsetails it is green, There are also variations between species in the number of leaf sheaths and stem ridges, and whether and how much the stems are branched. In Water Horsetail (*Equisetum fluviatile*), for instance, the stems are most commonly unbranched. and there are 10-30 ridges, whereas Marsh Horsetail (*Equisetum palustre*) is usually branched, though often sparsely, and has 4-12 ridges.

As shown in the widespread Common Horsetail (*Equisetum arvense*), the most obvious reproductive bodies are cones of sporangia, in which the spores are lodged. They are on separate unbranched stems which complete their work before the foliage stems appear. Each cone consists of densely packed whorls of stalked peltate discs called sporophylls on a central axis. The sporangia are below the sporophylls.

Horsetails adapt to a variety of environments. Common Horsetail can inhabit dry locations, whereas Giant Horsetail requires more moisture in the soil, though it can tap resources well below the surface. Marsh Horsetail is found in bogs, fens, marshes, wet heaths, woods and meadows, so needs to be adapted to wet places. Its creeping rhizome helps to stabilise it in swampy ground and its stems of up to two and a half feet enable it to compete with the other tall vegetation found in wet places. Further, it often forms subterranean runners and tubers, with which it can proliferate vegetatively. Survival is helped by its being poisonous to herbivorous animals It stem has a central cavity and a number of other spaces running down it, which helps oxygen and carbon dioxide to travel easily between the waterlogged underground parts and the aerial parts where interchange with the air can take place. It holds its cones above other vegetation in bogs and hay meadows to facilitate dispersal of spores by wind. Water Horsetail prefers standing water.

Giant Horsetail - teeth and ridges

Common Horsetail - fertile stems

cone showing sporangia

Water Horsetail - plant with unbranched stem

teeth and ridges

Marsh Horsetail - plant with branched stem

teeth and ridges

PLATE 58: FERNS

The only visible major structures in ferns are the leaves, which are called fronds. They arise from a rhizome which, in different species, is short or long and underground or on the surface. They emerge coiled into a spiral covered with protective scales and then unroll and expand. The range of frond structures is shown opposite. The overall outline can taper from a broad central area to both tip and base, have its sides roughly parallel or taper from broad base to tip. In some species, it is simple (undivided), as in Hart's Tongue (*Asplenium scolopendrium*), while in others it is divided, some once, as in Maidenhair Spleenwort (*Asplenium trichomanes*), others twice and a few three times, as in Male Fern (*Dryopteris filix-mas*), Broad Buckler Fern (*Dryopteris dilatata*) and Lady Fern (*Athyrium filix-femina*). In Rustyback (*Asplenium ceterach*) the division is pinnatifid, and the arrangement of the divisions is alternate. Where divisions are in opposite pairs, their arrangement on the frond is once, twice or thrice pinnate. The basic segments are called pinnae, divisions of pinnae are pinnules and divisions of pinnules tend to be labeled more vaguely, often as segments. In some species the frond is once pinnate near the tip and two or three times pinnate lower down the stalk. In Bracken (*Pteridium aquilinum*) the pinnae are stalked. The last divisions of the frond can themselves be indented - with teeth blunt or with bristles in Soft Shield Fern (*Polystichum setiferum*) and spines in Hard Shield Fern (*Polystichum aculeatum*). Water Fern (*Azolla filiculoides*) is exceptional in having small floating fronds.

Ferns inhabit a variety of environments. The large leaves of Bracken allow it to photosynthesise sufficiently in the shade of trees, as well as surviving in the open. In drier areas it has moderate resistance to drought through the thick surface and rigidity of the leaf and its capacity for vegetative spread by rhizomes allows it to survive there despite the lack of the layer of water required for sexual reproduction. It is poisonous to animals, so can survive grazing. The huge number of very tiny light spores produced maximizes dissemination in any environment. Rustyback (*Asplenium ceterach*) thrives on limestone outcrops and pavement and walls, growing in cracks and crevices where its short stout rhizome holds it fast. The thick surface layer of the fronds and the thick scales, silvery at first and finally brown, on the undersides help it survive the occasional desiccation in this environment. The fronds further resist drought by bending their pinnae inwards and curling up so that they temporarily look like really dead fronds.

Male Fern - frond uncoiling

tapering above and below

Broad Buckler Fern - tapering from base

Hart's Tongue - simple frond

Maidenhair Spleenwort - once pinnate

Lady Fern - thrice pinnate

Rustyback - sides parallel

brown scales below

live brown fronds

Soft Shield Fern - bristles on pinnules

Hard Shield Fern - spines on pinnules

Water Fern - fronds among Duckweed

PLATE 59: REPRODUCTION OF FERNS

Many ferns reproduce vegetatively by rhizomes. Otherwise, the only easily observable reproduction is asexual by spores. In the majority of ferns the spores are found on the backs of the fronds, but in a few they are borne on separate structures. In these instances the fertile fronds have reduced pinnae or pinnules and little or no photosynthetic ability. They are generally quite upright in the centre of the plant and the level of subdivision of the frond is similar to that of the sterile fronds. Royal Fern (*Osmunda regalis*) is the most dramatic example, and Hard Fern (*Blechnum spicant*) has the same feature.

Where the spores are on the backs of the fronds, they are in stalked bodies called sporangia, usually visible with a hand lens, and the sporangia are gathered together in groups called sori, sometimes on the margins, as in Bracken (*Pteridium aquilinum*), sometimes more or less central and usually associated with the veins, as in Male Fern (*Dryopteris filix-mas*). They also vary in shape - almost round in Intermediate Polypody (*Polypodium interjectum*), long-rounded to oblong in Lady Fern (*Athyrium felix-femina*) and Wall Rue (*Asplenium ruta-muraria*), kidney-shaped in Male Fern and linear or at least long and thin in Hart's Tongue (*Asplenium scolopendrium*) and Bracken. In some species they are protected by a flap called the indusium, in others exposed.

Hard Fern - vegetative fronds **fertile fronds** **Royal Fern - fertile and vegetative fronds**

Hart's Tongue - sori oblong/linear

Bracken - sori linear on margins

Intermediate Polypody - sori circular

Male Fern - sori kidney-shaped

sori along veins

Lady Fern - sori oblong to oval

Wall Rue - sori oblong, showing sporangia

Male Fern - indusia and sporangia

PLATE 60: MOSSES

Mosses belong to a group of plants called bryophytes, which also includes liverworts. They are like ferns and horsetails in having neither flowers nor seeds and reproducing most conspicuously by spores, the sexual structures being minute. However, unlike ferns, the spores are always produced in structures separate from the leaves and there are no woody conducting tissues. Overall, they are low-growing plants with weak structure.

There are over 760 species of moss in Great Britain and Ireland. Most of them have no genuine vernacular names, and, until recently, bryologists have relied mainly on the scientific names. However, in the 2010 outstanding British Bryological Society guide to the group *Mosses and Liverworts of Britain and Ireland: A Field Guide* by Atherton, Bosanquet and Lawley, all main species are also given a popular name. Most are not very memorable and they are often confusingly similar to each other, so scientific names will mainly be used here.

Mosses typically have a stem which bears simple, delicate, leaves without stalks, but sometimes with a single visible vein. They are mostly spirally arranged, but occasionally opposite. They are usually rooted by delicate attachment threads called rhizoids. Mosses typically have a spore capsule on a stalk called a seta, but some have them very rarely and most have them only at certain times of year - mainly in the winter, the best time to study mosses. The spore capsule most commonly has a protective covering called a calyptra, a lid called an operculum and a set of teeth that control escape of the spores called a peristome.

There are many ways in which different moss species can be distinguished which require no artificial aids beyond a close-up lens - preferably one with built-in illumination. It is difficult to discern some of these features in dry conditions, when the plants are in a desiccated state. A small water-spray bottle will refresh them in seconds and overcome the problem.

Mosses on walls, rocks and other inhospitable surfaces often grow as small humps, impressive mounds or carpets, which helps protect them against exposure to cold winds and frost. By reducing the surface area relative to the overall bulk, it also cuts down water loss and it traps rainwater as a defence against desiccation. Those growing in woods tend to be larger and spreading or tall to give a large area for absorbing carbon dioxide for photosynthesis in an environment in which the lack of light tends to reduce it. The aquatic Willow Moss (*Fontinalis antipyretica*) has long spreading stems to reach as much water space as possible for the same purpose. Other mosses may have long tentacle-like stems. Looking more closely, there is a distinction between acrocarps, most of which grow upright and bear any capsules present at the tops of the stems, and pleurocarps, most of which form more or less prostrate branching wefts or mats with capsules arising from the sides of the main stems. If branched, they can have a tree-like appearance or be fairly regularly pinnate or bipinnate.

***Grimmia pulvinata* - hummocks on wall top**

***Tortella tortuosa* - mounds on wall top**

***Hypnum cupressiforme* - close mat**

***Anomodon viticulosus* - carpet with long stems**

pleurocarpous

***Polytrichum commune* - tall moss in wood**

***Kindbergia praelonga* - pinnate**

***Thamnobrum alopecurum* - tree-like**

***Atrichum undulatum* - acrocarpous**

Willow Moss - colony in pond

branched stems

PLATE 61: LEAVES OF MOSSES

Leaf characters are useful for distinguishing mosses. Leaves are mostly spirally arranged, but some are in two opposite rows. They can be broad or narrow. Some have colourless, white or grey or silvery tips or hairs, usually associated with exposed habitats such as wall tops or rock faces, where they trap a layer of moist and relatively warm air close to the plant. Leaves can be curved or straight, and have a visible nerve or not, and nerves sometimes protrude beyond the end of the leaf. In some species there are flat strips of green tissue on the nerve making it especially prominent. Leaves of some species contort into a spiral when dry and are not immediately recognisable as the same species, or may just curl up - both helping to conserve moisture by reducing the surface area and trapping such moisture as remains. Many species can become totally desiccated and cease to function and later absorb water and come back to life.

In the aquatic Willow Moss (*Fontinalis antipyretica*) the leaves are folded along the middle and each has a sharp keel along the centre, which makes them look like boats, a shape which allows water to flow past them without causing them any harm. Woodland mosses often have large or numerous leaves to maximize photosynthesis in the limited light.

Willow Moss - spiral, no visible nerve

***Fissidens taxifolius* - two rows, central vein with short point**

***Neckera complanata* - leaves broad, transparent, two rows with no central nerves**

Atrichum undulatum **- undulate, green strips over veins**

Rhynchostegiella tenella **- very narrow**

Barbula convoluta **- spiral, long**

Homalothecium sericeum **- silvery with long terminal points**

curled up when dry

Hypnum cupressiforme **- leaves with long curved bristle at end**

Tortella tortuosa **- long, wavy-edged and twisted**

contorted into spiral when dry

Tortula ruralis **- broad, silvery hairs, nerve**

PLATE 62: REPRODUCTION IN MOSSES

Everyday observation of mosses allows one to look only at their reproduction by spores. Sexual reproduction is carried out by tiny male and female structures and does not directly produce new individuals. Instead, it produces spore capsules whose spores are then dispersed mainly by the wind to produce new plants. In *Fontinalis antipyretica*, the spores can also be dispersed in the water.

The form of the capsule and its stalk the seta are frequently diagnostic. The capsules can be held clear of the leaves on long setae or nestle among or near the leaves. The former enhances the possibility of wind dispersal, but the protected position is better in harsh environments, such as wall tops or rock faces. The capsules can be erect, inclined to one side or drooping, and variously coloured. They have a variety of shapes, sometimes including a terminal projection called a beak. In many species, each has a lid called an operculum which takes a variety of forms, and a temporary loose hood called a calyptra covers it early on and persists longer in some species than in others. In *Encalypta vulgaris* the calyptra forms a translucent hood surrounding the capsule. Most species have a system of teeth called a peristome which can open and close to control the escape of spores, but a few do not. In some species, such as *Tortula muralis*, the capsules are individually enveloped in glistening water droplets after rain.

Setae can be of different lengths and colours. They are red or purplish in some species, but green to yellow in others or when young. Some species, such as *Brachythecium* species, have minute projections called papilla on the setae.

Some species also reproduce vegetatively. In *Funaria hygrometrica* (Common Cord Moss) new plants can develop almost anywhere on its surface. In *Tortella nitida*, the tips of the leaves can fall or be nipped off and grow into new plants. *Fontinalis antipyretica* can reproduce from stem fragments.

Tortula muralis **- mature capsules erect, obvious calyptras, long setae yellow-green to reddish**

capsules in water drops

Common Cord-Moss - reddish setae, capsules hanging, beaked

***Brachythecium rutabulum* - long red setae, capsules inclined, curved, black, opercula, peristomes**

***Rhynchostegium confertum* - long red setae, capsules curved, peristomes**

***Bryum capillare* - long red setae, green capsules hanging till ripe**

***Schistidium crassi-pilum* - capsules erect, red, among leaves**

***Grimmia pulvinata* - capsules green, among leaves on bent down setae**

***Orthotrichum anomalum* - setae short, green to to yellow to brown, capsules red-brown, ridged**

***Encalypta vulgaris* - translucent hoods over capsules**

***Polytrichum commune* - capsule 4-angled**

PLATE 63: THALLOSE LIVERWORTS

There are approaching 300 liverwort species in Britain and Ireland. Like mosses, they are bryophytes, low-growing plants with no woody conducting tissues and neither flowers nor seeds and reproducing most conspicuously by spores, the sexual structures being too minute to study without a microscope. As with mosses, the best identification guide is the one by Atherton and others and species are referred to here by their scientific names.

Liverworts, like mosses, usually have their bodies rooted to a surface by rhizoids and, typically but not universally, have a spore capsule on a stalk called a seta. However, some liverworts differ from mosses in not having stems with leaves, the plant body consisting of a broad flat plate called a thallus. Liverwort capsules tend to have setae weaker and more transparent than those of mosses and the capsules are usually shorter-lived, and therefore rarely seen, and do not have the calyptras, opercula or peristomes found in mosses.

Liverworts divide fairly neatly into thallose species such as *Conocephalum conicum* and leafy species such as *Plagiochila asplenioides*, with a small group of intermediates. Some thallose species are just flat plates in shape, though variously lobed at the margins, while others are narrow and elongated or in rosettes.

Reproductive structures are hard to find in most species. However, *Marchantia polymorpha*, displays its male and female organs on stalked, flat-topped discs, the male with short rounded lobes and the females with finger-like lobes. In *Conocephalum conicum,* purple cushions can sometimes be seen near the apex and these bear the male reproductive organs. *Marchantia* also bears scattered cups containing disc-shaped asexual bodies called gemmae. Raindrops falling into a cup can eject gemmae up to 50cm from the parent and thus bring about their dispersal. Asexual bodies also occur in other species.

Among other characteristics useful for distinguishing species are the fragrant smell when *Conocephalum conicum* is bruised, and the hexagonal markings in that species, which have pores in the centre which lead to air chambers, which presumably allow carbon dioxide to get to the green parts inside quickly. *Marchantia* also has pores, seen as white dots, with air chambers beneath.

***Conocephalum conicum* - part of colony on wall beside watercourse**

broad thalli with white markings

white markings close up

***Conocephalum conicum* - lower surface with rhizoids**

site of male organs

***Metzgeria furcata* - long narrow forked thalli**

***Marchantia polymorpha* - thalli with gemmae**

white dots and gemmae close up

sites of female organs

PLATE 64: LEAFY LIVERWORTS

Leafy liverworts are superficially similar to mosses. However, the leaves are more often very thin and frequently transparent and lack the central vein which can be seen in many mosses, and they are sometimes deeply lobed, which does not occur in mosses. A stem bearing spirally arranged leaves indicates a moss, whereas liverworts have them in two opposite rows, sometimes with another row beneath. However, some mosses also have them in opposite rows, though without an additional row.

Leafy liverworts are, like thallose liverworts, mainly flat. There are two opposing rows of leaves, but this can be obscured by additional features. In *Porella platyphylla*, for instance, each leaf in the basic two rows is divided into a large upper lobe and a smaller lower lobe, and there is an additional row of larger leaves underneath, conspiring to give the impression that there are five rows. The structures overlap to such an extent that it is difficult to make out the details - as the photo shows. In other species leaves may have three, four or many lobes. It has too be seen as an achievement just to recognize something as a leafy liverwort.

As with thallose liverworts, reproductive structures are hard to find. Indeed, some species may not have them - identification books do not, for instance, mention them for *Porella platyphylla*, and it may be that it reproduces mainly by detached fragments. In *Plagiochila asplenioides* capsules are produced only rarely.

Other characteristics helpful in distinguishing species include the translucent sheen of the leaves of *Plagiochila asplenioides* and their small marginal teeth.

***Plagiochila asplenioides* - leafy stem**

leaves overlapping in 2 rows from above (left) and below

***Porella platyphylla* - colony on dry stone wall**

close up view

***Porella platyphylla* - upper and lower leaf surfaces, the lower (right) with each lateral leaf divided into a large and small lobe and a central additional row of leaves**

PLATE 65: GREEN ALGAE

Algae are now mostly agreed to be outside the Plant Kingdom and their study is separately labeled as phycology or algology. This is despite having characteristics typical of the plant kingdom - most of them do not move about actively like animals, they consist of one or more cell-like structures with cellulose walls and the cells have bodies in them called chloroplasts which contain chlorophyll to catalyse photosynthesis. The issue is still debated and it is not impossible that some of the algae might be reinstated as plants.

At least 5,000 species of algae are claimed for Great Britain and Ireland. They are distinguished from other plant-like organisms largely by their simple structure. Their tissues are not organized into distinct organs, such as stems, leaves, roots, and rhizoids. Sexual reproduction occurs in most species, but not to the naked eye, and some also produce asexual spores, which often have whip-like flagella with which they swim to a new location. Vegetative reproduction is also common, often just by fragmentation.

There are three main groups of algae - Green Algae, Red Algae and Brown Algae, now commonly put into three different kingdoms. They range from tiny single-celled bodies to quite complex multicellular forms. Unicellular green algae can be seen only in the mass. Tiny, free-floating algae give pond water its characteristic green color, while other species are seen as green coatings on tree trunks, rocks, walls, paths, boards and so on, highly resistant to desiccation. In some green algae, the cells are joined together to form filaments, as in *Trentopohlia* species on tree trunks, where the green of the chlorophyll is masked by an orange pigment, and in Blanket Weed, where this structure allows them to congregate in strands or masses just below the surface of ponds to receive as much sunlight as possible. Some other species occur as two to thousands of cells embedded in gelatinous strands or spheres.

Green seaweeds include more complex forms, and can be found in rock pools attached at their bases to rocks, pebbles or other seaweeds or, in a few cases, free-floating, or detached and washed up on to sand and shingle beaches. Examples are *Enteromorpha linza* and *Ulva lactuca* (Sea lettuce). The former has membranous, spirally twisted fronds with crinkled edges which appear flat but are really hollow tubes, and can be up to 20 inches long, so that they can float freely to give maximum access to the light and carbon dioxide, particularly when the tide comes in. The latter has a thin flat frond.

The British Phycological Society supports identification books, such as the highly technical *The Freshwater Algal flora of the British Isles*, edited by David John and others. The *Collins Complete Guide to British Coastal Wildlife* by P. Sterry and A. Cleave has a selection of photographs of common seaweeds. *A Field Guide to the British Seaweeds* by Emma Wells, with a key and illustrations, is available online at the time of writing - it's best to search for it.

Single-celled algae - mass on fence

Trentopohlia

Filamentous alga - colony in garden pond

Filamentous alga - filaments

Green, red and brown algae - in rock pool (Photo John Roberts)

Green, red and brown algae - on shingle

***Ulva lactuca* - thin flat frond**

***Enteromorpha linza* - view**

spirally twisted frond

crinkled edges

PLATE 66: RED ALGAE

Like green seaweeds, red seaweeds can be found in rock pools attached at their bases to rocks, pebbles or other seaweeds or, in a few cases, free-floating. Specimens washed up on to sand and shingle beaches may still be attached to visible or buried rocks or pebbles or to other seaweeds. Though they contain chlorophyll and photosynthesise, the chlorophyll is masked by pigments of other colours, making the organisms pink, red, reddish brown or purple.

Like seaweeds generally, the red species are mostly in the intertidal zone and must adapt to alternate submersion and exposure and the strong action of the waves. Their structures reflect this. Some species form a crust on some surface or other, while others have a more specific structure ranging from thallose to tubular to filamentous, and often branched. Frilly or wavy edges are found in some species, as are small marginal projections. Some species have a distinct midrib and some side veins. Some are thin, delicate and translucent, others thick and leathery. Most have an attachment called a holdfast, which can be an adhesive disc or an assembly of processes forming a claw shape. Reproductive structures are rarely visible without a microscope, but *Callophyllis laciniata* has small projections along the surface on which reproductive bodies form.

Polysiphonia furcellata provides a good example of how these organisms are adapted to the tidal environment. It can be seen at any level on the beach and in rock pools. Its delicate, feathery branched filaments enable it to float easily in the water to be near light and air and to allow fast moving water to flow past it easily rather than damaging or detaching it. It has a claw-like holdfast which attaches it to and helps avoid its being swept away from rocks, other algae, mussels or limpets and artificial substrates. The red pigments in red algae generally are particularly effective in absorbing the green and blue-green light in deeper waters, so some species can survive there.

Crust-forming - on submerged rocks (Photo by John Roberts)

Callophyllis laciniata **- crimson, thick, flat, highly divided, fan-shaped, wide fronds, small projections, disc holdfast**

Cryptopleura ramosa **- thin, flat, pinkish, broad, frilly branches, wavy**

Dilsea carnosa **- dark red to brown, thin, flat, tough, leathery, several stalked fronds**

disc holdfast

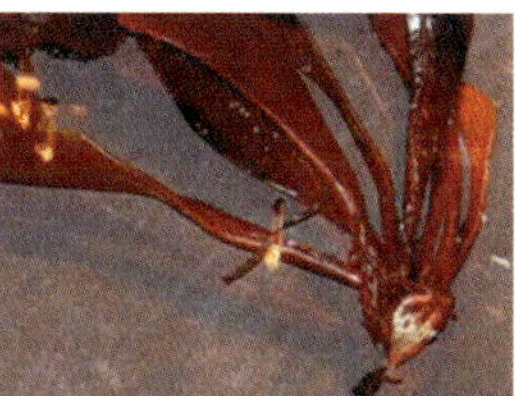

Membranoptera alata **- pinkish, thin branched stalks forking into flattened, thin lobes**

Palmaria palmata **(Dulse) - purple to blackish, thick flat lobes much branched**

marginal blades

Furcellaria lumbricales **- dark red to brown, thin long cylindrical tubes**

Furcellaria lumbricales **- cylindrical tubes**

claw holdfast

Polysiphonia **species - pink, branching filamentous, feathery**

Polysiphonia **species - feathery filaments**

claw holdfast

PLATE 67: BROWN ALGAE

Brown seaweeds occur in much the same places as green and red seaweeds. Their chlorophyll is masked by pigments which make the organisms brown or olive in colour. Like seaweeds generally, the brown species are mostly in the intertidal zone and must adapt to the alternation of submersion and exposure and the strong action of the waves. The best known are tough to withstand wave action and have a powerful holdfast and sometimes a basal stalk-like structure called a stipe. Some species have air-filled bladders to keep the body afloat for maximum access to sunlight to promote photosynthesis. Their size is, on average the greatest of the three main groups, with giant species that grow to 7 metres in Britain. In some species reproductive areas can be distinguished.

Bladder Wrack (*Fucus vesiculosus)* is a good example of adaptation to the intertidal zone. It has large flattened fronds called laminae which are up to three feet or more long and have a strengthening midrib with air bladders in pairs along each side of it. It is attached to rocks or other surfaces by a disc-shaped holdfast. These features, enable it to survive even where the waves are quite rough, and to float freely when the tide comes in so that it can be as near the light and air as possible and not get buried under shifting sand or tangled up with other vegetation. It is elastic in texture, which enables it to yield to wave action rather than resisting it and getting detached from the surface. Survival on the open shore while the tide is out is helped by its tough outer surface to restrict water loss and its water-retaining mucilaginous structure. Swollen fruiting bodies with a granular surface occur at the tips of branches. They bring about sexual reproduction through male bodies which swim through the water to fertilise the female organs. Bits can also break off and grow into new individuals asexually. These methods allow extensive colonization of shores.

Knotted Wrack (*Ascophyllum nodosum*) is long and narrow, forks repeatedly and has bladders along the middle. *Fucus serratus* has toothed edges and a distinct midrib. *Laminaria digitata* has large, thick, wide, flat fronds, split into finger-like lobes, and a distinct smooth stipe.

Bladder Wrack - colony

group with flat branching fronds

midrib, bladders and fruit bodies

Knotted Wrack - narrow, bladders central ***Fucus serratus*** **- midrib, toothed** ***Laminaria digitata*** **- wide lobes, stipe**

PLATE 68: STONEWORTS

Some authorities say stoneworts, also known as charophytes, are plants, others green algae. They have a more complex structure than other algae, with an erect stem-like structure, and many whorls of short linear branches reminiscent of the horsetails at the nodes. Thalli are attached by rhizoids to sandy or silty substrates in quiet, shallow, fresh or brackish water and range from a few centimeters to several decimeters in height. In calcium-rich water they become stiff and lime-encrusted. Though there are several hundred species worldwide and over 30 in the British Isles, they are not often seen, partly because they are very susceptible to pollution. They are mostly annuals, and can reproduce by fragmentation or by vegetative outgrowths, as well as sexually and by spores, and can colonise new ponds rapidly. There are two genera, *Chara* with undivided branches and *Nitella* with forked ones, and the photo here looks like a *Nitella*. There are a number of species of each which are difficult to distinguish. The *Botanical Society of Britain and Ireland* has published a guide to identification of the group - *Charophytes of Great Britain and Ireland* by Jenny Moore.

Nitella **species - in garden pond**

close up

PLATE 69: FUNGI

Fungi used to be regarded as primitive plants. Now, however, their area of study is referred to as mycology rather than botany and there are three separate kingdoms for former "fungi". This plate and Plates 70-84 cover the kingdom of "true fungi". They are best identified by their scientific names, and only well-established English names are used here.

Unlike plants, the body structure of fungi consists of filamentous structures called hyphae with walls mainly of chitin, also found in the surface of insects. The hyphae grow in living organisms or dead remains by secreting chemicals which break down the complex organic substances into simple ones which they then absorb, so there is no photosynthesis and therefore no chlorophyll. The hyphae of a fungus are collectively called the mycelium. Normally you can't see the hyphae, but a photo shows a hand lens view in *Rhizopus nigricans*, where they come above the strawberry surface. It also shows fruit bodies, which are spherical sporangia. These, as in the observable reproductive bodies of fungi generally, protrude above the surface so that the spores they contain can be dispersed mainly by the wind when the containing structure bursts opens.

At least 12,000 species of fungi are known in the UK. Their classification depends on microscopic characters, so here they are grouped according to easily seen characteristics, mostly of fruit bodies, which do not always put related species together. In the best-known fungi, fruit bodies are made up of masses of intertwined hyphae which produce spores in an area called the hymenium.

The groups here are: recognised only by their effects on the host; fruit bodies flat on a wood surface (resupinate), sometimes projecting at the top like a shelf; fruit bodies rounded projections on the host surface; fruit bodies incorporating a spherical or pear-shaped body; fruit bodies disc- or cup-shaped (cup fungi); fruit bodies cylindrical or club-shaped; fruit bodies of irregular shape; fruit bodies with a central stalk called a stipe and a cap on top with radiating vertical strips called gills on the underside (agarics); fruit bodies in the form of a horizontal bracket projecting from the host surface with radiating vertical strips called gills on the underside (agarics); fruit bodies with a central stalk called a stipe and a cap on top with pores on the underside (boletes mostly); fruit bodies horizontal brackets projecting from the surface with pores on the underside (bracket fungi); fruit bodies with a central stalk called a stipe and a cap on top, or a bracket, with teeth, spines or pegs covering the underside (tooth fungi).

Recently published identification guides are *Collins Complete Guide to British Mushrooms and Toadstools* by Paul Sterry and Barry Hughes and *Collins Fungi Guide* by Stefan Buczacki. The more technical *Collins Field Guide to Mushrooms and Toadstools of Britain and Europe* by R. Courtecuisse and B. Duhem is available second hand. Photos can be found online. Fungus forays are organized through British Mycological Society groups and other organizations.

***Rhizopus nigricans* - hyphae**

***Phragmidium violaceae* - host effects**

***Stereum rugosum* - resupinate**

***Hypoxylon fuscum* rounded bumps**

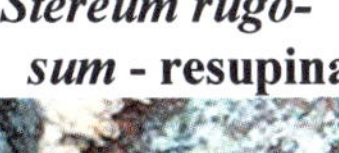

***Scleroderma verrucosum* - (Earthball) - spherical**

***Clavulinopsis fusiformis* - cylindrical**

***Sarcoscypha austriaca* (Scarlet Elfcup) cup fungus**

***Tremella mesenterica* (Yellow Brain Fungus) - irregular**

***Calocybe carnea* - agaric**

***Crepidotus variabilis* - bracket-shaped agaric**

***Boletus edulis* (Cep) - bolete**

***Inonotus dryadeus* - bracket**

underside with pores

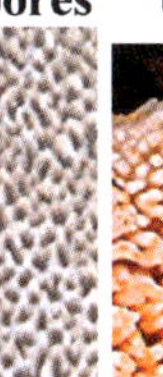

***Hydnum repandum* - underside with teeth**

PLATE 70: FUNGI RECOGNISED BY EFFECTS ON THEIR HOSTS

Fungi parasitic on plants grow in the host tissues and do not always have obvious fruit bodies. Tar spot (*Rhytisma acerina*) reproductive bodies, for instance, look like colorations on the surface of the Sycamore leaf. Their dark areas break open in spring to show a green disk from which the spores escape. Apple Scab (*Venturia inaequalis*) has distinctive dark scabby spots on leaves and fruit on traditional apple trees and the spores erupt through them.

Two major groups of parasitic fungi are the rust and smuts. *Phragmidium violaceae* is a rust with the reddish brown spore areas with violet margins and white dead areas on bramble leaves seen in Plate 69, and another phase when it produces blotches of yellow spores. *Melampsora* species are rusts which produce yellow spore masses on willows. Anther Smut of Red Campion (*Ustilago violaceae/Microbotryum violaceum*) has spores which turn the anthers dark purple.

Other effects on host plants include many other discolorations, galls and other abnormal outgrowths, distortion, wilting, shriveling of leaves and death.

Tar spot (*Rhytisma acerina*)

***Melampsora* species**

Phragmidium violaceae

Anther Smut of Red Campion

Apple Scab

PLATE 71: FUNGI WITH FRUIT BODIES FLAT (RESUPINATE), USUALLY ON WOOD, SOMETIMES PROJECTING

Stereum rugosum, which grows on dead wood, has been shown in Plate 69. The spore-producing hymenium is on the upper surface of the resupinate part and the lower surface of the bracket. *Byssomerulius corium* is similar but often entirely flat and the hymenium is on the exposed surface and is at first smooth, then wrinkled into a network of grooves which have the spores on their surface.

Byssomerulius corium - on a dead log **hymenium**

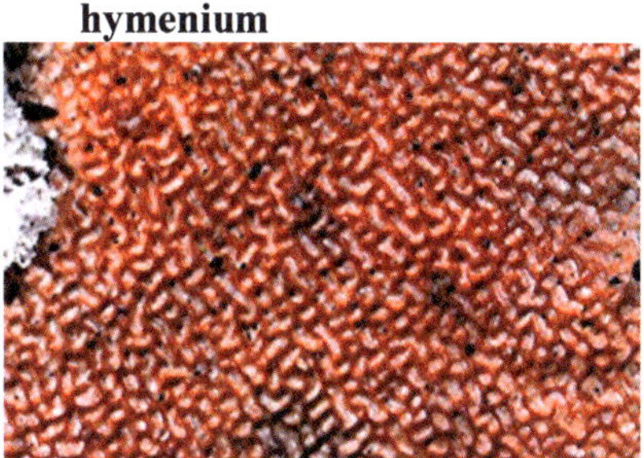

PLATE 72: FUNGI WITH FRUIT BODIES ROUNDED PROJECTIONS

One of these is Coral Spot Fungus (*Nectria cinnabarina*), with pink to orange to reddish brown fruit bodies about a millimeter across and globular to cushion-shaped on dead fallen twigs or small branches. Another is the larger Cramp Balls or King Alfred's Cakes (*Daldinia concentrica*) also on dead fallen wood, with fruit bodies irregularly globular and up to about 10cm across. New surfaces form on top of old ones, so you get a series of concentric rings, all formed in one season. Some species can be identified only by their host tree. For instance, a number of species in the genus *Hypoxylon* look much like *Hypoxylon fuscum* in Plate 69, but different species grow on the dead wood of different trees. This one is found on Hazel or Alder, while other species occur on Beech, Birch and Ash. All these species have the hymenium at the surface and spores are shot out from it.

Coral Spot Fungus **King Alfred's Cakes - group** **section to show concentric rings**

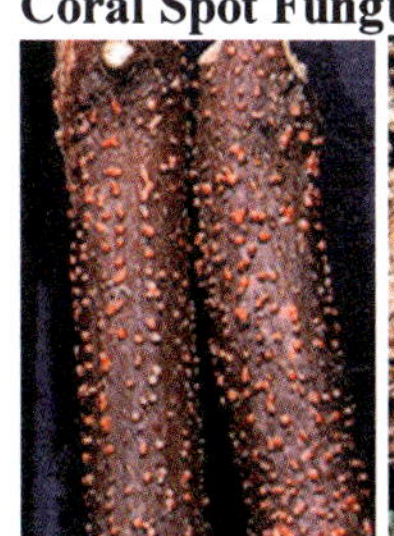

PLATE 73: FUNGI WITH FRUIT BODIES SPHERICAL OR PEAR-SHAPED, RELEASING SPORES FROM INSIDE

Earthballs, such as *Scleroderma verrucosum* in Plate 69, are so named because the fruit bodies are on soil. They are up to about 7cm across and the spores are in a powdery mass inside and released by splitting open or decay of the fruit body wall and then dispersed by the wind. Giant Puffball (*Calvatia gigantea*) behaves similarly, but is off-white in colour and has circumferences up to over 5 feet and, before splitting, pressure on it can produce jets of powdery spores. One fruit body can produce 7 billion spores. Puffballs, such as Stump Puffball (*Lycoperdon pyriforme*), open by a pore at the top. When the surface is prodded, by a raindrop for instance (or by your finger), a cloudy mass of spores can be seen emerging. It grows on dead wood, usually stumps, is pear-shaped and up to about 6cm tall. Earthstars, such as *Geastrum triplex,* are up to about 11cm across on the ground, and the fruit bodies have two layers of wall. The outer wall splits open into segments and the exposed inner sac opens by apical pores.

Giant Puffball

Earthstar (*Geastrum triplex*)

Stump Puffball - from the side

from above to show the apical pore

PLATE 74: FUNGI WITH FRUIT BODIES CYLINDRICAL OR CLUB-SHAPED

The spores of this group are borne on or in the fruit body surface and the spores are shot out to catch the wind. Some of them are simple cylinders like some specimens of Dead Man's Fingers (*Xylaria polymorpha*), which is up to about 8cm long on dead wood and is sometimes branched. Its spores are in surface pits. Others are club-shaped, like the Scarlet Caterpillar Fungus (*Cordyceps militaris*), which parasitizes pupae and larvae of butterflies buried in soil and produces spores on the inner walls of hollow projections with a terminal pore. The much larger Stinkhorn (*Phallus impudicus*), famous for its appalling smell, is on the ground, but usually attached to dead wood by thick underground cords of hyphae called rhizomorphs. It can be up to about 20cm tall and is shaped like a human penis, as its name *Phallus* indicates. The cap is covered by smelly olive green mucus which is eaten by flies, together with the spores in the hollows of the cap. The spores pass through the fly's digestive system unharmed to bring about dispersal.

The remaining examples here produce their spores on the surface. Candlesnuff Fungus (*Xylaria hypoxylon*), also on dead wood, can be single or branched and up to about 6cm high. Its spores are produced on the powdery white tips. Fairy clubs grow on the ground, mainly saprophytic on dead plant litter and mainly between 12 and 30cm high. Some have single simple fruit bodies, narrowly cylindrical in *Macrotyphula phacorrhiza*, and club-shaped in *Clavariadelphus pistillaris*. Others are clustered, such as Golden Spindles (*Clavulinopsis fusiformis*) shown in Plate 69. Coral fungi are branched, as in *Ramaria stricta*.

Dead Man's Fingers

Stinkhorn

Clavariadelphus pistillaris

Ramaria stricta

Scarlet Caterpillar Fungus - on buried chrysalis

Candlesnuff Fungus

Macrotyphula phacorrhiza

PLATE 75: FUNGI WITH FRUIT BODIES DISC- OR CUP-SHAPED

Cup fungi grow mostly on dead wood, feeding on it saprophytically. The fruit body is cup-shaped, often becoming disc-shaped, and the diameter is mostly up to about 5cm. The hymenium is on the inside or upper surface, and the spores are shot out from it. *Peziza varia* is an example in which the stages of opening can be seen. Black Bulgar (*Bulgaria inquinans*) is another. Some are colourful, such as Scarlet Elf Cup or Orange Peel Elf Cup (*Sarcoscypha austriaca*) in Plate 69, which grows on the ground and is bright orange red, and Green Wood Cup (*Chlorosplenium/Chlorociboria aeruginascens*). Some species prefer particular trees. For instance, both Black Bulgar and Green Wood Cup particularly invade oaks, the former also favouring Beech, the latter staining the wood blue.

***Peziza varia* - on timber early**

on timber later

Black Bulgar - on dead branch

Green Wood Cup - wood stained blue

PLATE 76: FUNGI WITH FRUIT BODIES OF IRREGULAR SHAPE

There are many fruit body shapes which approach the unique. One is Jew's Ear (*Auricularia auriculae-judae*) which is up to about 8cm across, is saprophytic on dead Elder and often looks like a human ear. Its relative Tripe Fungus (*Auricularia mesenterica*) looks like tripe. Also on wood, up to 8cm across, but parasitising the mycelium of another fungus, is Yellow Brain Fungus (*Tremella mesenterica*), shown in Plate 69, which looks like a human brain. In these species the hymenium is on the surface. In the saprophytic Bird's-nest Fungus (*Cyathus striatus*) the spores are in egg-like structures called peridioles, which are inside a cup and each attached to it by a fine thread which can be up to 18 cm long. A raindrop bounces off the bottom of the cup and sweeps them up with it - or the fruit body swells and explodes when wet, catapulting the peridioles and threads a metre or more, the threads unwinding as they go and finally breaking off at the base. Being tacky, a thread sticks to some object, the periodoles hanging from it. The spores are released only when the periodole walls are destroyed by insects or otherwise.

Odd shapes are also found in fungi with fruit bodies on the ground. Morel (*Morchella esculenta*), has one up to about 20cm high and is folded and convoluted like a sponge, with spores forming in the surface in the pockets.

Dry Rot (*Serpula lacrymans)* grows saprophytically inside coniferous wood in buildings, but also usually produces an external mass of fluffy threads. Within this mass, dark cords called rhizomorphs develop which can travel over non-nourishing materials to reach a place where further infection becomes possible. The cords can pass through mortar or pores in bricks or even stone or under cement floors or plaster.

Jew's Ear - single fruit body

on a dead stump

Tripe Fungus

Bird's-nest Fungus - on mossy log

fruit body

Dry Rot - fruit body

Dry Rot - fluff and rhizomorphs

Morel - fruit body

convolutions

PLATE 77: FUNGI WITH A STIPE, CAP AND RADIATING GILLS

These fungi, known as agarics (see *Calocybe carnea* in Plate 69), are usually soft-bodied and vary from minute to 30cm or more high, with caps from very tiny to 30cm or more across. The gills are, on average, about 0.5-0.7mm apart. The spores form on the sides of the gills and, when ripe, are shot horizontally about 0.1 mm, then fall downwards and get blown away by the wind. A four inch cap of a mushroom would produce about 100,000,000 spores per hour.

There are all sorts of other ways of telling gill fungi apart, of which the type of gill attachment is crucial. Free gills are not attached to the stipe and lie well clear of it. Adnexed gills are also unattached but lie close to the stipe. Adnate gills are attached to the stipe and join it more or less at a right angle. Some attached gills have an upward indentation just before the attachment then come down again to join the stipe, and they are called sinuate. If they are indented but don't come down again they are sometimes called emarginate. Finally, the gills of some species join the stipe and run down it, and they are called decurrent.

Overall shapes are much used in identification, but these overlap and can change as a fruit body develops. The shapes are associated with the gill attachment. The collybioid shape has a stipe of medium breadth, a flat or slightly convex cap and adnate or sinuate gills. The tricholomoid shape has a thicker stipe, convex and fleshy cap and adnate or sinuate gills. The clitocyboid shape has a thick fleshy stipe and a concave, sometimes funnel-shaped cap and decurrent gills. The mycenoid shape has a thin and often delicate stipe and a small, conical or bell-shaped cap. Some species have a cap which is very thin and sometimes transparent and sometimes turned up at the edges. Another feature is a central hump on the cap called an umbo. The stipe is usually cylindrical and sometimes broader downwards, often with a swollen "bulb" at the extreme base.

A number of identification details reflect fruit body development. They are almost fully formed underground, but need to absorb water and expand to reach mature form. Each fruit body starts off like a little bulb, with a covering called a veil. The veil breaks open during the expansion, and leaves bits of itself on the fruitbody which are diagnostic. There can be remnants of one or both of two kinds of veil. A partial veil attaches the edges of the cap to the stipe and breaks off to leave fragments on the cap edge, and/or radiating fibrils called a cortina connecting the cap edge to the stipe and/or shaggy projections or a complete ring on the upper part of the stipe. A universal veil covers the whole of the young fruit body and breaks to leave loose patches on the top of the cap and torn bits or an encircling bag called a volva round the base of the stipe.

English names used as labels for photos are Brown Rollrim (*Paxillus involutus*), Buttercap (*Collybia butyracea*), Plums and Custard (*Tricholomopsis rutilans*), Panther Cap (*Amanita pantherina*) and Deathcap (*Amanita phalloides*).

Pluteus cervinus **- free gills**

Hygrocybe chlorophana **- adnexed**

Hygrocybe **species - adnate**

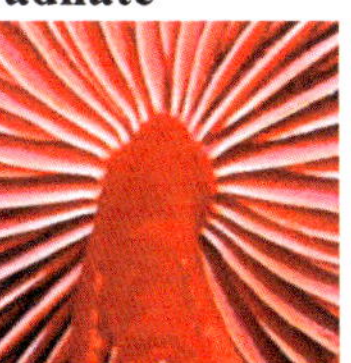

Tricholoma alba **- sinuate**

Brown Rollrim - decurrent

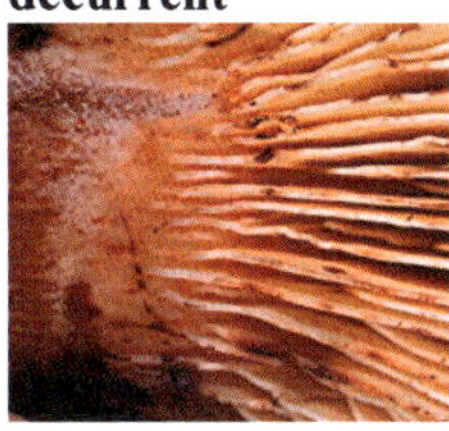

Buttercap - collybioid

Plums and Custard - tricholomoid

Clitocybe geotropa **- clitocyboid**

Mycena haematopus **- mycenoid (conical)**

Bolbitius vitellinus **- mycenoid (bell)**

Coprinus lagopus **- thin transparent cap**

Panther Cap - universal veil on cap, partial veil ring

Deathcap - volva from universal veil

Armillaria gallica **- cortina from partial veil**

PLATE 78: OTHER AGARIC SHAPE FEATURES

The nature of the ring is diagnostic. It is very obvious in Parasol Mushroom (*Macrolepiota procera*), where it often can be moved up and down the stipe. Sometimes the ring hangs downward as in *Amanita pantherina* (Panther Cap) in Plate 77, whereas in others it can be horizontal or even directed upwards, as in *Agaricus xanthodermus* (Yellow Stainer). A number of species of *Agaricus* have marks underneath the ring giving the effect of a cogwheel. Sometimes the ring is double.

There are some features which are characteristic of groups of species or genera. The consistency of the flesh is one of these. For instance there's a group sometimes called the Brittle Caps (*Russula* species), which fall apart easily, as well as having white gills. By contrast waxcaps, (*Hygrocybe and Hygrophorus* mainly), which also have white gills, have firm flesh. Other groups have fibrous stipes - when you try to break the stipe it just separates into tough threads, while others break cleanly. Another group characteristic is the presence of latex in the cap which exudes when the cap or stipe is broken. If this happens, the specimen is usually a species of *Lactarius* - the milkcaps, as in *L. fulvissimus*. Their flesh is fragile, like *Russula* species, but the latter don't exude latex. Some species of *Mycena* also exude latex, such as *Mycena haematopus*, where it is dark red (Plate 77). Many of the inkcaps are so named because they use a process called autodigestion for recycling nutrients. A soon as the spores are dispersed, the caps start to dissolve from the edges into a black liquid, and eventually disappear, as in *Coprinus picaceus* (Magpie Inkcap).

There are also characteristics which are specific to particular species rather than to genera. Scales of various kinds occur on the cap and/or stipe of some species. Shaggy scales are attached to the cap in *Pholiota squarrosa,* rather than loose as in *Amanita* species (Plate 77). Radial striations which sometimes develop into splits occur in *Inocybe rimosa*, glistening spicules when young in *Coprinus micaceus*, transparency in *Coprinus lagopus* (Plate 77) and a woolly covering in *Lactarius torminosus* (Woolly Milkcap). For stipes, some bear longitudinal lines, which is described as fibrillose, as in Buttercap (*Collybia butyracea*), some are powdery as in *Bolbitius vitellinus*, some have a surface with a snakeskin pattern as in Parasol Mushroom, and it helps to know if the stipe breaks gradually and irregularly or whether it is brittle and breaks more or less straight across in one go - audibly in *Mycena vitilis.*

Many fungi are said to be recognisable by their smells or tastes. The Aniseed Toadstool (*Clitocybe odora*), for instance, does actually smell of aniseed. In *Lactarius* the latex of some species tastes bitter and of others not.

Parasol Mushroom - loose ring, snakeskin

Yellow Stainer - cog wheel

***Agaricus* species - double ring**

***Lactarius fulvissimus* - latex exuding**

Magpie Inkcap - fruit body

autodigestion

***Pholiota squarrosa* - scales**

***Inocybe rimosa* - striations and splitting**

Glistening Inkcap - glistening spicules

Woolly Milkcap - woolly

Buttercap - striations on stipe

***Bolbitius vitellinus* - stipe powdery**

PLATE 79: COLOURS OF AGARICS

The colour of the cap and stipe is often helpful for telling fungi apart. For instance, in the genus *Russula* the caps have different and often very striking colours. The photos show bright red in *R. emetica* (The Sickener, with a burning hot taste), dark red in *R. xerampelina*, purple in *R. drimeria*, brownish yellow in *R. ochroleuca* and black (after a white start) in *R. nigricans*. Stipes come in a variety of colours, many the same as the cap, as in *R. drimeria*, but sometimes different, as in many other Russula species, where a white stipe commonly contrasts with the coloured cap. Stipe colour can also vary at different levels, as in *Mycena inclinata*, which is at one stage whitish at the top, orange in the middle and dark brown at the base. Some fungi reveal particular colours when cut open. Yellow Stainer (*Agaricus xanthodermus*), for instance, reveals chrome yellow flesh in the basal bulb of the stipe.

One of the most useful features for identifying agarics is the colour of the spores. Though they cannot be seen individually, they are usually sufficiently abundant to colour a surface on which they fall, and the colour is different in different genera. It can be shown by cutting the cap from the stipe, placing it underside down on a flat surface and covering it with a piece of plastic or other material which will reduce water loss and enable it to retain its shape. After a few hours, the cap is lifted carefully off the paper and radiating bands of colour can be seen where the spores have fallen down between the gills. The result is called a spore print, and the colours shown include brown, pink, purple, black in Weeping Widow (*Lacrymaria lacrymabunda*), white in Fairy Ring Champignon (*Marasmius oreades*) and purple in Sulphur Tuft (*Hypholoma fasciculare*). People do not always agree on how to label some colours - some pinks can be confused with some browns, for instance - so it is best to think fairly broadly when using this characteristic.

Gill colour is also helpful and most commonly reflects the colour of the spores - both are normally white in *Rusula* - but not always. Sometimes the colour is not uniform. In *Panaeolus* species, such as Bell-shaped Mottlegill (*P. campanulatus*), they are mottled due to uneven development of the spores. In *Mycena pelianthina* there are interrupted dark purplish edges.

Russula emetica ***R. xerampelina*** ***R. drimeria***

R. ochroleuca

R. nigricans

***Mycena inclinata* - stipes**

Yellow Stainer - yellow at cut base

Kuehneromyces mutabilis

Galerina praticola

Weeping Widow

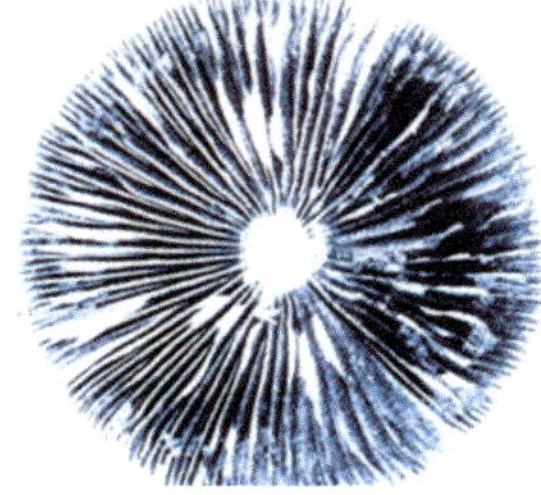

Fairy Ring Champignon

Pluteus cervinus

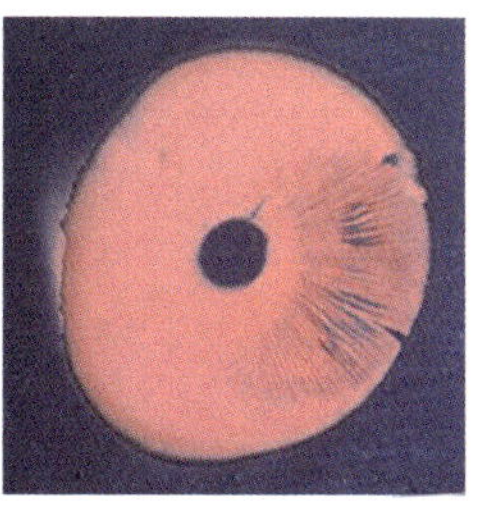

Sulphur Tuft - spore print and gills

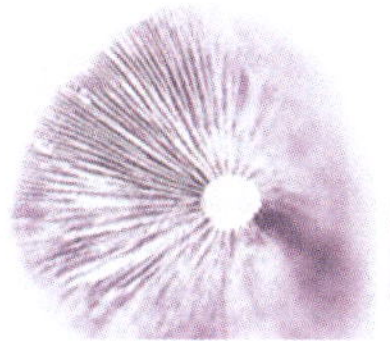

Bell-shaped Mottlegill - mottled gills

***Mycena pelianthina* - dark at gill edges**

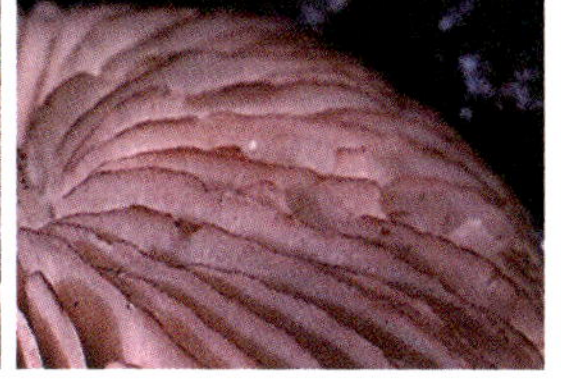

PLATE 80: THE HABITATS OF AGARICS

In some fungi identification is helped by their habitat. Many whose fruit bodies are found on the ground beneath trees regularly patronise specific species. This is because they form associations with tree roots called mycorrhiza which help the tree absorb nutrients from the ground while also feeding the fungus. Thus, Fly Agaric (*Amanita muscaria*) is normally found beneath Pine or Birch, while its relative the Deathcap (*Amanita phalloides*) grows mainly under broad-leaved trees, especially Oak. Many fungi on dead wood of trees are also associated with particular trees or tree groups. Winter Fungus or Velvet Shank (*Flammulina velutipes*) is most common on dead elms. On the other hand, Honey Fungus (*Armillaria mellea*) occurs on both broad-leaved and coniferous trees. It's a parasite and a saprophyte, continuing to live on the tree after it has killed it and spreading from tree to tree by thick cords of hyphae called rhizomorphs. A variety of species are found growing saprophytically on other woodland constituents - *Marasmius epiphyllus* is found on dead leaves, *Marasmiellus rameales* on dead twigs, *Mycena haematopus* on dead stumps or logs and Conifer Conecap (*Baeospora myosura*) on buried cones.

Many fungi are found almost entirely in grassland, such as the *Hygrocybe* species referred to elsewhere. Some of the field dwellers are on dung, such as *Annellaria semiovata.* Certain species, such as *Galerina pumila,* grow amongst moss, though it is not necessarily clear what the relationship is.

The arrangement of fruit bodies on the accommodating surface is another aspect of habitat identification. They can be borne singly, or in troops, as in Fairies' Bonnets (*Coprinus disseminatus*) or in groups joined at the base as in *Psathyrella candolleana*. The fruit bodies of a number of species, mostly soil-living species, occur in rings (called fairy rings). The mycelium grows outwards in all directions from its point of initiation and the fruit bodies come up at the margins of the area covered, as in St George's Mushroom (*Calocybe gambosum*).

Fly Agaric - with fallen Birch leaves

Winter Fungus on dead Elm

***Mycena haematopus* - on a dead stump**

Honey Fungus -

on a tree it has killed

rhizomorphs

***Marasmiellus rameales* -**
- on dead twigs

***Marasmius epiphyllus* -**
on dead leaves

Conifer Conecap -
on a cone

***Annellaria semiovata* -**
on dung

***Galerina pumila* -**
in moss

***Psathyrella candolleana* -**
cluster near stump

Fairies' Bonnets -
in a troop on a dead stump

St George's Mushroom -
in a ring on a lawn

PLATE 81: EDIBLE OR POISONOUS?

Any fungus can poison people when it has begun to decay. A smaller number are poisonous when fresh. Poisonous species can easily be mistaken for edible ones without specialised knowledge. Top of the poisonous list is the Deathcap (*Amanita phalloides*) (Plate 77). Half a cap can kill. A relatively small number of species run the Deathcap close, though deaths in this country are now rare.

Most poisonous fungi cause only mild or transitory upsets. Fly Agaric (*Amanita muscaria*) (Plate 80), for instance, can induce excitement, hallucinations, deep coma and awakening to forgetfulness and sometimes headaches, and sometimes colic, vomiting and diarrhoea, convulsions and sleepiness. Recovery is rapid, and in some parts of the world, such as Siberia, it's been used recreationally (like alcohol) or in religious ceremonies. So has the Bell-shaped Mottlegill (*Panaeolus campanulatus*) (Plate79*)*, which can promote exhilaration followed by semi-consciousness, delirium and hallucinations. The Yellow Stainer (*Agaricus xanthodermus*) (Plates 78 and 79), whose general appearance is not unlike that of a number of edible species of *Agaricus,* can cause stomach upsets. The Common Inkcap (*Coprinus atramentarius*) has been used to cure alcoholism, because chemicals it contains combine with alcohol to make one feel sick within a few moments. Other poisonous agarics include Poison Pie (*Hebeloma crustuliniforme*), *Clitocybe dealbata* and Sulphur Tuft (*Hypholoma fasciculare*). The photos show how inoffensive some of them can look.

Collecting and eating fungi has a strong following. The wild Mushroom (*Agaricus campestris*) has long been collected. Shown here, Shaggy Inkcap (*Coprinus comatus*), Wood Blewits (*Lepista nuda*) and Horse Mushroom (*Agaricus arvensis*) are in the top twenty edible fungi collected, and also favoured are St George's Mushroom (*Calocybe gambosa*), Shaggy Parasol (*Macrolepiota rhacodes*), *Lepiota excoriata*, Wood Mushroom (*Agaricus silvicola*), *Clitocybe geotropa* (Plate 77), *Lepista flaccida*, Blewits (*Lepista saeva*), *Hygrocybe pratensis*, Blusher (*Amanita rubescens*), *Pluteus cervinus*, Goblet (*Pseudoclitocybe cyathiformis*), Amethyst Deceiver (*Laccaria amethystina*), *Kuehneromyces mutabilis* and *Entoloma clypeatum.* Species which are eaten but can disagree with some people are Honey Fungus (*Armillaria mellea*) (Plate 80), and Clouded Agaric (*Clitocybe nebularis*).

POISONOUS

Common Inkcap

Poison Pie (Photo by John Roberts)

Sulphur Tuft

Clitocybe dealbata

EDIBLE

Horse Mushroom

Shaggy Inkcap

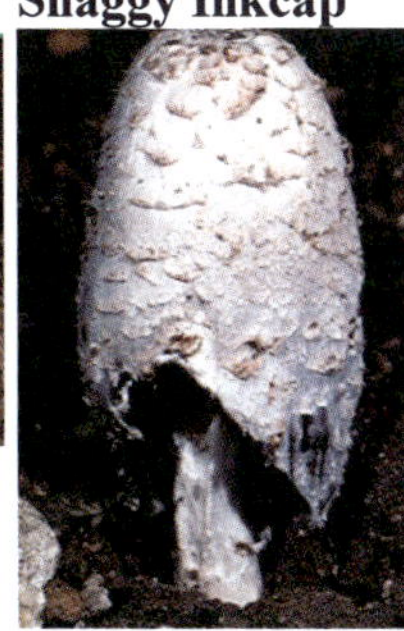

St George's Mushroom

Shaggy Parasol

Clouded Agaric

Wood Blewits

Blusher

Goblet

Amethyst Deceiver

Lepista flaccida

Entoloma clypeatum

Blewits
(Photo by John Roberts)

PLATE 82: FUNGI WITH A CENTRAL STIPE AND A CAP ON TOP WITH PORES ON THE UNDERSIDE

The boletes are included here, fitting the category exactly. The cap is mostly up to about 20cm across and is on top of a stipe up to about 15cm long. It has, instead of gills, vertical tubes which open by pores at the lower end, as shown in Red-cracked Bolete (*Xerocomus chrysenteron*). The spores form on the surface of the tubes and are propelled to a distance which gets them to the middle of the tube, so that they can fall out of the pores and get blown away by the wind. The shape of the pores helps identification. In Red-cracked Bolete and *Suillus bovinus* they are large, angular and irregular, whereas in Bay Bolete (*Boletus* or *Xerocomus badius*) they are also large and angular but have a tidier appearance. In *Leccinum carpini* they are small and a large proportion are round.

The colour of the pore-bearing undersurface also differs from one species to another. In *Leccinum carpini* it is whitish at first, then grey yellow, in Bay Bolete (*Boletus* or *Xerocomus badius*) it is at first cream and later greenish yellow, while in *Suillus bovinus* it is orange brown. In some species the pore-bearing surface changes colour if bruised. For instance, Bay Bolete is distinguished from Cep/Penny Bun (*Boletus edulis*) (Plate 69) by its turning blue when touched. Red-cracked Bolete also bruises blue, but not so much. *Leccinum carpini* bruises black. The spores can be different colours, though spore prints are not often taken with this group. One is shown for Red-cracked Bolete.

Some species, usually referred to as polypores, have the division into cap and stipe less marked, as in *Polyporus leptocephalus* (= *varius*), *found on* dead or dying deciduous trees.

Most boletes are mycorrhizal and are found in association with trees. A species may associate with a variety of trees as in the Cep, or with one or a few species. *Suillus grevillei* (Larch Bolete), for instance, is usually found under Larch.

Boletes are well known for being good to eat - except the few poisonous species. Both Cep/Penny Bun Bolete and Bay Bolete are in the top twenty edible fungi collected in Britain for personal use by enthusiasts. Red-cracked Bolete is edible but mushy when cooked.

Red-cracked Bolete - fruit body

vertical section of cap showing tubes

pores

Suillus bovinus **- pores large, angular, irregular**

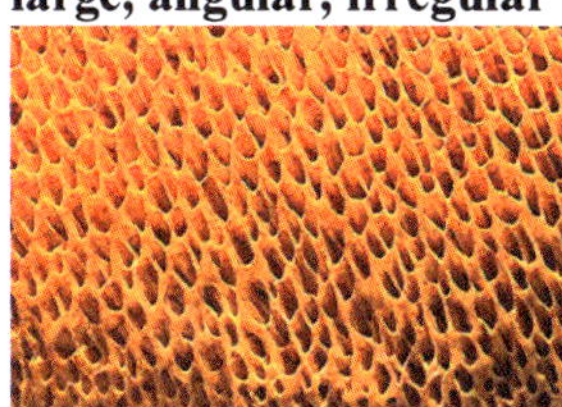

Bay Bolete - pores large, angular

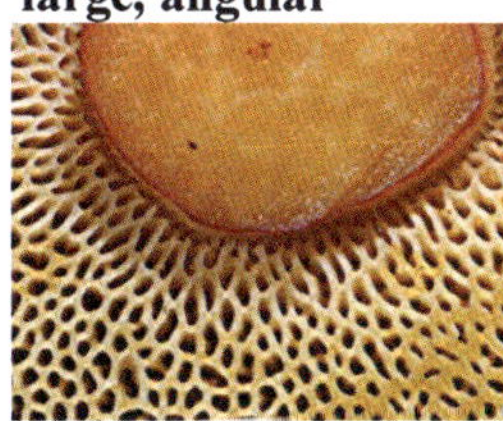

Leccinum carpini **- pores variable, mostly round**

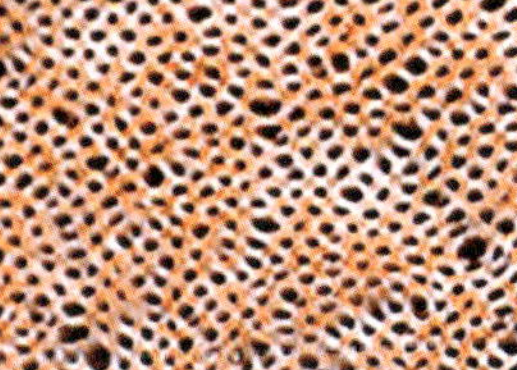

Bay Bolete - fruit body with blue bruising

Red-cracked Bolete - spore print

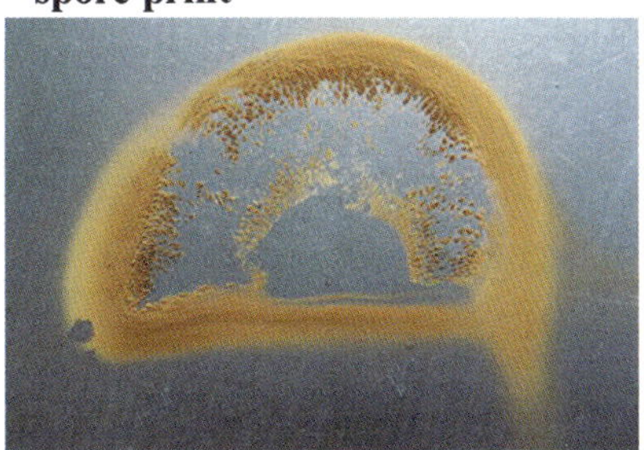

Polyporus leptocephalus - fruit body

Larch Bolete

PLATE 83: FUNGI WITH HORIZONTAL BRACKETS AND PORES ON THE UNDERSIDE

These are called polypores or bracket fungi. An example is Beefsteak Fungus (*Fistulina hepatica*), which is parasitic on Chestnut and Oak. Its bracket, up to 25cm across, comes straight out of the tree trunk or a branch, usually on the lower part of the trunk. The paler underside bears the hymenium. A cross section shows why it is called the Beefsteak Fungus, and also shows the vertical tubes of which the hymenium consists. Each tube opens on to the undersurface by a pore and dispersal is the same as for species with caps and pores.

Different bracket fungi differ from each other in the size, shape and colour of the fruit body, whether it is borne singly or as part of a group or tier, the size and shape of the pores and the kind of tree or wood it grows on. They can be a few centimetres across or huge, bulky or thin and flat, and soft-bodied or tough. The photos show upper surfaces which are darkish red, grey-black, brown with a white edge, zoned ochre and brown with a paleish edge, pale brown mottled with dark brown markings, and, in Many-zoned Polypore (*Trametes versicolor*), with concentric bands of different colours, sometimes so attractive that they have been made into brooches or earrings. Undersurfaces shown are whitish, cream to ochre, and purplish red bruising brownish red, but they can change with age. You can draw pictures on that of Artist's Fungus (*Ganoderma australe* and other species) with any pointed implement. The tubes and pores hang separately from each other in Beefsteak brackets, but are more commonly joined by the bracket flesh. Pores are variously of different sizes and shapes - angular, round, slit-like or maze-like and can be close together or widely separated. Some species have soft fruit bodies which function for a very short time, like the Beefsteak Fungus, which stops producing spores before it goes hard. Others have very tough and sometimes perennial fruit bodies, like the Artist's fungus, which can last 20 years or so and produce a new layer of spores each year.

Many bracket fungi are found only on dead stumps, trunks and branches, some on deciduous and some on coniferous. Beefsteak Fungus is on living oaks, while Razor-strop Fungus/Birch Bracket (*Piptopterus betulinus*) and Artist's Fungus attack and kill live trees and then continue to live saprophytically on the dead wood. Razor-strop Fungus is restricted to one type of tree - Birch.

Beefsteak Fungus - on Oak trunk **fruit body section** **tubes separate**

Beefsteak Fungus - pores separate

Razor-strop Fungus on fallen dead Birch

Many-zoned Polypore - tiers, concentric bands

Artist's Fungus - tier on dead Beech

artist's under surface

pores very small, round, distant lyspaced

***Daedaleopsis confragosa* - on dead fallen branch**

under side, purplish with brownish bruising

some pores round and some slit-like

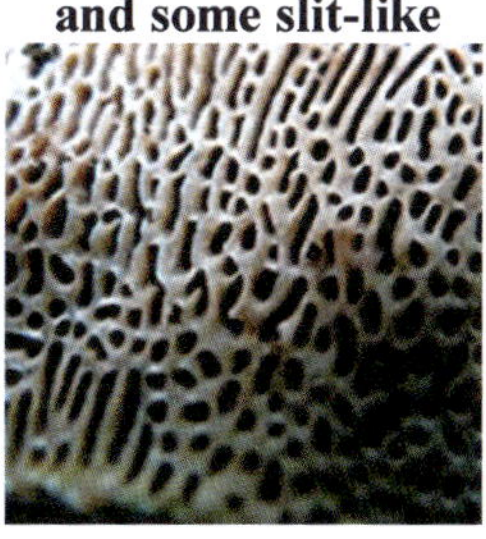

Dryad's Saddle (*Polyporus squamosus*) - on deciduous stump

pores large and angular

Oak Mazegill (*Daedalea quercina*) - pores maze-like

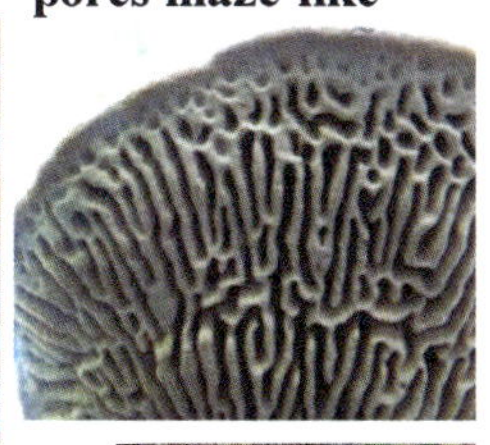

Hoof Fungus (*Fomes fomentarius*) - on dead wood of deciduous tree, single, grey-black, hoof-shaped

PLATE 84: CRUSTOSE LICHENS

A lichen is a fungus with green algae or cyanobacteria or both living inside it. Cyanobacteria are organisms with some resemblances to algae and were formerly called blue-green algae. The fungus feeds on carbohydrates produced by the algae or cyanobacteria during photosynthesis and they derive protection from physical damage and desiccation from being inside the fungus, and probably mineral salts and water which the fungus has absorbed from the soil. Partnerships of this kind between two living organisms which are to the benefit of both parties are called symbioses or symbiotic associations. Here, however, the fungus and its partner combine in a way that makes them like a single organism. The algae or cyanobacteria can, if necessary, live on their own without the fungus, whereas the fungi involved are not known outside lichens. Lichens grow very slowly, sometimes only adding a few millimeters to their size in a year, but they can have very long life spans. One has been found in the Arctic that is more than 4,500 years old. There are at least 1,700 species of lichen in Britain and Ireland. Help with the difficult process of identifying them is available from local lichen recorders appointed by The British Lichen Society and its local groups that organise forays. The Society also publishes various leaflets to help identification. Collections of lichen photos can be found by searching online. Frank Dobson's *Lichens: An illustrated Guide to the British and Irish Species* (6th edition, 2011) is comprehensive, with many photos.

The body of a lichen is called the thallus. In lichens with algae, it usually has upper and lower layers of fungal hyphae with a layer of single-celled algae between. In lichens with cyanobacteria, the thallus is usually gelatinous with the cyanobacteria scattered about in it. The underside is attached to a surface either directly or by thread-like outgrowths called rhizinae. The overall shape of lichen thalli takes a number of forms. In crustose lichens, it's a broad thin layer flat on a surface, sometimes inside it and usually difficult to separate from it. This is ideal for survival in such inhospitable environments as the surfaces of walls, exposed rock surfaces and tree trunks. The flat bodies attached to the surface minimise exposure to wind and cold. Since they have very thin bodies and grow slowly, they make few demands on supplies of nutrients in an environment where these are hardly present. Further, lichens generally can remain alive in a totally dehydrated condition for a year of more until they are able to reabsorb water and become rejuvenated. They can also cope with extremely high and extremely low temperatures. A conspicuous example of a crustose lichen is *Caloplaca aurantia*, which has a golden yellow thallus mainly on the exposed tops of walls. *Aspicilia calcarea*, also on wall tops, is smooth and white to pale grey, with cracks that divide it into areas called areoles, which look like islands. *Diploicia canescens* has its margins divided into lobes (a condition which has been referred to as placodioid). *Rhizocarpon geographicum* on rocks and *Lecidella elaeochroma* on trees have a map pattern, because young individuals don't join up when they meet but form a black no-man's-land between them.

Sexual reproduction occurs only in the fungus part of a lichen and the bodies which are dispersed as a result of it do not contain any algae or cyanobacteria. It results in the production of spores (sometimes referred to as conidia) which get carried away by wind and grow into new lichens if they find a new alga or cyanobacterium to rely on. In *Caloplaca aurantia*, the spores are in round flat deeper orange discs called apothecia (singular apothecium) or ascocarps. In *Aspicilia calcarea* each areole has one or more irregularly shaped, dark brown to black apothecia sunk below the surface. *Lecanora campestris*, also on walls, has large, dark brown apothecia with whitish margins crowded in the centre. *Lecidella elaeochroma* has convex, black to dark red apothecia, while *Graphis scripta* has them long and narrow and sometimes branched. *Acrocordia conoidea*, on walls, has its spores in closed, black, conical and prominent flasks called perithecia.

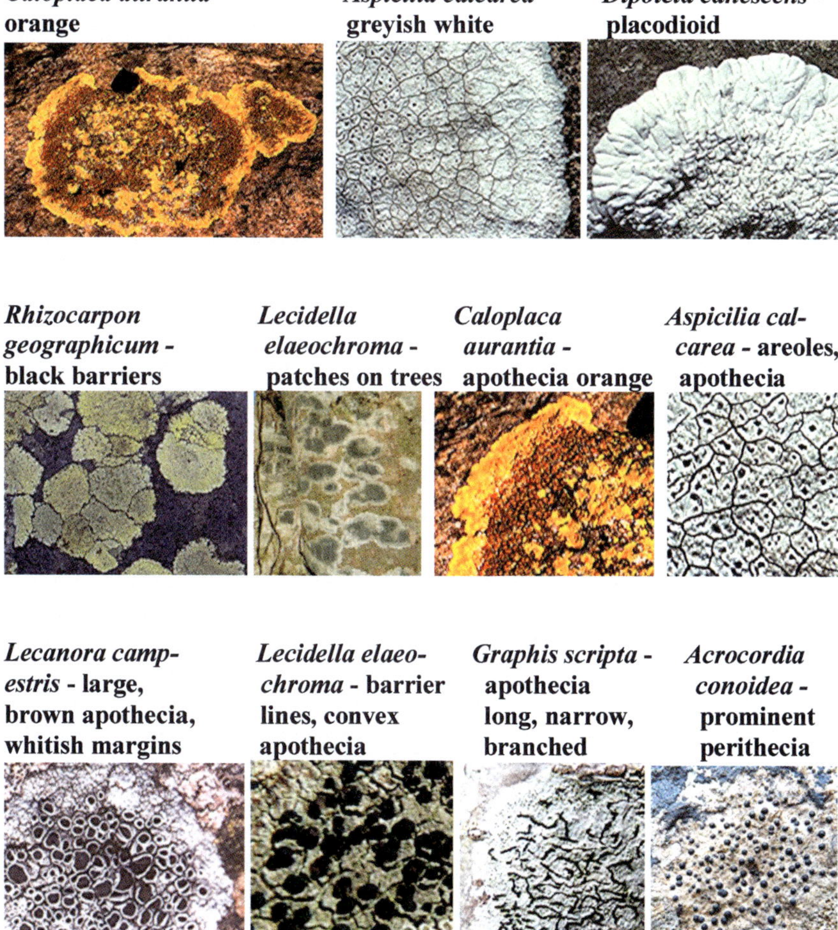

***Caloplaca aurantia* - orange**

***Aspicilia calcarea* - greyish white**

***Dipoicia canescens* - placodioid**

***Rhizocarpon geographicum* - black barriers**

***Lecidella elaeochroma* - patches on trees**

***Caloplaca aurantia* - apothecia orange**

***Aspicilia calcarea* - areoles, apothecia**

***Lecanora campestris* - large, brown apothecia, whitish margins**

***Lecidella elaeochroma* - barrier lines, convex apothecia**

***Graphis scripta* - apothecia long, narrow, branched**

***Acrocordia conoidea* - prominent perithecia**

PLATE 85: FOLIOSE LICHENS

Foliose lichens have a leafy structure, with lobes raised above the surface. One of the commonest is *Physcia adscendens,* which grows on rocks or tree bark. It has a thallus divided into lobes up to 1mm wide raised at the tips and with long marginal hair-like threads called cilia. Another growing in similar habitats is *Flavoparmelia caperata,* which has a thallus up to 20cm across which is grey when dry but green when wet. The lobes are up to 1cm wide and wrinkled and contorted when mature. *Xanthoria parietina* on walls, tree branches and twigs is greenish grey in shade but bright orange when exposed to strong sunlight. It has long wrinkled lobes, which can be prostrate or upright. In *Peltigera membranacea* the anchoring rhizinae can be seen easily. *Collema auriforme* is typical of lichens with cyanobacteria as the partner of the fungus in having a jelly-like consistency, swelling up when wet, which is useful for water retention on the tops of walls on which it is found. Foliose lichens generally are low-growing to help survival in dry or exposed conditions, but thrive most when there is nourishment in the surface on which they grow - either because rock fragments and dead bits of other living things have combined to produce a primitive soil or where bird droppings have enriched the surface.

This is a useful group for looking at reproductive bodies in lichens, which can be sexual or asexual. Asexual reproduction in lichens involves a part of the fungus and some of the algal or cyanobacterial cells forming either a small outgrowth called an isidium (plural isidia) or powdery granules called soredia (singular soredium) which break off from the main lichen body and are transported by wind, water, or animals. When one of them reaches a resting place, it can grow into a new organism. The sexual bodies called apothecia are obvious in *Peltigera membranacea* and *Xanthoria parietina.* In *Collema auriforme*, reproduction is mainly asexual by isidia, which are small coarse globular structures just about visible through a hand lens on the upper surfaces of the squamules. In *Flavoparmelia caperata*, the surface becomes covered in coarse asexual soredia, which are grouped together in areas called soralia. In *Parmelia sulcata* the surface becomes covered with a faint white network of ridges called pseudocyphellae, along which soralia eventually develop. In *Punctelia subrudecta*, the soralia develop from dot-like pseudocyphellae.

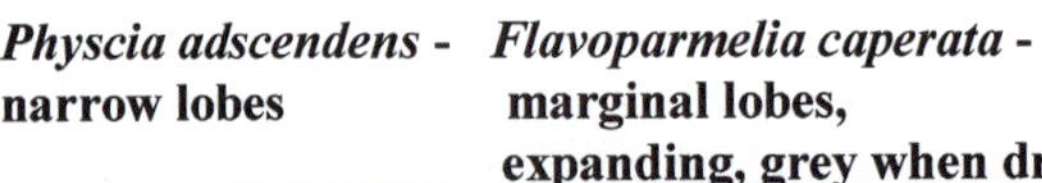

***Physcia adscendens* - narrow lobes**

***Flavoparmelia caperata* - marginal lobes, expanding, grey when dry**

green when wet

***Xanthoria parietina* -**
colony on wall

***Peltigera hymenina* -**
olive green, shiny, apothecia red-brown

***Peltigera membranacea* -**
grey-white thallus, long rhizinae

***Collema auriforme* -**
brown jelly-like lobes

***Peltigera membranacea* -**
apothecia

***Xanthoria parietina* -**
wrinkled lobes, apothecia

***Flavoparmelia caperata* -**
soralia and soredia

***Parmelia sulcata* -**
linear pseudocyphellae

***Punctelia subrudecta* -**
soredia, dot-like pseudocyphellae

PLATE 86: LEPROSE, SQUAMULOSE AND FRUTICOSE LICHENS

In addition to crustose and foliose, lichens can be filamentous, leprose, squamulose or fruticose. Filamentous lichens are not often seen by amateur naturalists. Leprose lichens are in a loose powdery mass. *Lepraria incana*, for instance, on walls, consists of fluffy greyish green granules which often become enveloped in a network of fungal hyphae. Fruit bodies are unknown.

Squamulose lichens are composed, at least in part, of tiny, overlapping scales called squamules. In *Cladonia coniocraea,* on bark or decaying wood, these are bright green. Squamulose lichens often have vertical tubular structures called podetia which usually bear some kind of reproductive bodies. These are cylindrical and slightly tapering in *Cladonia coniocraea* but funnel-shaped in *Cladonia pyxidata* (Chalice Moss), a wall species. It is said that spores are dispersed by raindrops which drop into a podecium and bounce out again, taking spores with them. The reproductive bodies can be sexual or asexual. In *Cladonia coniocraea* asexual soredia are found on the upper part of the podetium, both inside and out. The sexual apothecia are also borne on podetia in some species - not in *Cladonia pyxidata*, but clearly in *C. floerkeana* (Devil's Matches), where they are intensely red in colour. Asexual bodies can also be seen in squamulose lichens without podetia. *Caloplaca citrina*, on walls, is made up of minute squamules which become covered in granular soredia, so that it looks leprose. *Candellaria reflexa*, which grows on trees, has small granules or squamules which quickly become covered with soredia that look like small fluffy balls.

Fruticose lichens have long narrow lobes which can grow on the ground or on branches. On branches, they may hang like a straggly beard, or grow upright, when they look like small shrubs. *Ramalina farinacea* has a thallus of pale green rather flattened branches up to about 3mm wide and 5cm long, and often with sides raised so the centre is like a channel. The branches all arise from a common anchorage called a holdfast. Floury-looking soredia occur along the margins in roundish soralia. *Usnea cornuta* provides a more dramatic example, with a thallus which is pale green to grey with a waxy blue tinge and is tufted to half-hanging. The main branches are stout and somewhat shiny, with many finer side branches. The main branch bears small white dots on which develop isidia and soredia. Less common because it is seriously affected by air pollution is *Usnea ceratina,* which also has a grey-green thallus, but has its branches hanging down for up to about a metre. Fruticose lichens thrive, and can become quite large in cool shady environments like woods where water is not so easily lost, and where a larger surface area for photosynthesis is helpful because of the lack of light. Many of them are vulnerable to atmospheric pollution, so are not found near urban areas.

Lepraria incana - leprose

Cladonia coniocraea - green squamules, cylindrical podetia

Cladonia pyxidata - grey squamules, funnel-shaped podetia

Cladonia floerkeana - red apothecia on podetia

Caloplaca citrina - squamulose, looking leprose

Candellaria reflexa - fluffy squamules

Ramalina farinacea - fruticose, flattened branches

Usnea cornuta - fruticose with shorter hanging branches and *Usnea ceratina* with longer ones

Usnea cornuta - branches

white dots

PLATE 87: SLIME MOULDS

Slime moulds takes different forms at different stages of their life history. When food is plentiful, they can be unicellular with a single nucleus inside a mass of protoplasm which moves around and feeds on bacteria and fungi by flowing round and engulfing them, just like the Amoeba of school biology textbooks. When food becomes scarce, they amalgamate into slimy jelly-like masses called plasmodia with many nuclei, which continue to feed in an amoeboid manner. So they are more like animals than fungi or plants, and are placed in a kingdom including amoeba-like organisms and green algae - called the Protista or Protoctista. They flow over or through rotten wood or bark or dead leaves and twigs, often at speeds beyond 10 cm per day. They eventually transform themselves into fruit bodies, which contain the spores, which when dispersed develop into new individuals.

In *Trichia decipiens* the fruit bodies are called sporangia. The white bases of these in the photo are parts of the plasmodium which will soon transform themselves into sporangium stalks. In some species the stalk can be very distinct and long - as in the unidentified species shown. The fruit body is not always a simple sporangium. Sometimes it consists of a collection of closely packed sporangia, which are still individually recognizable, called a pseudoaethalium, as in *Tubifera ferruginosa,* which occurs on wood, preferring coniferous, or *Mucilago crustacea* on herbaceous stems or woody twigs. In some other species, the fruit body consists of a mass called an aethalium in which the individual sporangia are unrecognizable, as in *Lycogala terrestre.* These various fruit bodies do not rise as much as a centimeter above the surface.

***Arcyria denudata* - fruit bodies with shed spores**

***Trichia decipiens* - fruit bodies and remains of plasmodium**

Unidentified slime mould - long sporangium stalks

***Tubifera ferruginosa* - pseudoaethalium**

***Mucilago crustacea* - pseudoaethalium on a twig**

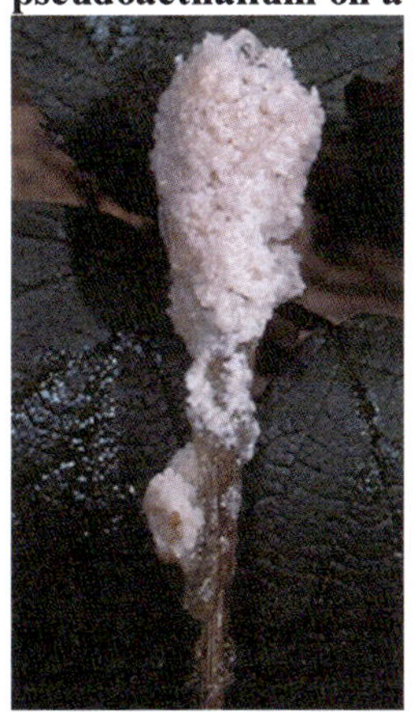

close up

***Lycogala terrestre* - aethalium**

close up

PLATE 88: ECOLOGY AND GRASSLAND

Plants live in communities, along with other living organisms. The study of communities is called ecology. It involves how individual plants are adapted to their environments, which was covered in Plates 43-47, and how plants and other organisms live together in communities, described in this and following plates. A community may also be referred to as an ecosystem. Community types can be named according to broad categories such as grassland, or more precisely, as in the *National Vegetation Classification* (*NVC*) described by John Rodwell and his co-workers (1991-2006) in five volumes. Thus grassland dominated by the grass Upright Brome (*Bromopsis erecta*) they call *Bromopsis erecta* grassland (CG3). Plants particularly characteristic of a type of community are called indicators or axiophytes.

Basic (alkaline) and acid soils have different assemblages of plant species and there are differences between the basic chalk and limestone versions. Mountain grassland is different from lowland grassland. Meadows used for grazing are different from those used for hay. Climate can affect what grows. For instance, Wood Cranesbill (*Geranium sylvaticum*) occurs in grassland in the North, but is virtually unknown in the South.

Perhaps the most studied grasslands are those that occur on limestone - a range of rocks which contain at least 50% of calcium carbonate and includes chalk. Soils on limestone are called calcareous and are alkaline, porous so that they drain well, dry, well-aerated and warm. There may, however, be periods of drought. They may be grazed or cut for hay, or left to themselves. The ways in which a wide range of plants are adapted to these conditions is explained in Plate 44. Here, a brief account is given of the composition of the communities.

In any community, there are usually dominant species which are more abundant than others and often affect the growth of others. In grassland they are normally grasses. On limestone, they are often either Upright Brome (*Bromopsis erecta*) or Tor Grass (*Brachypodium pinnatum*). Their companions have to be plants which can grow through the grass mat or on periodic bare patches and compete with it. Firstly, there are plants called calcicoles which, because of their chemistry, cannot cope with acid conditions and are rarely found elsewhere than on alkaline soil. Plate 1 shows Stemless/Dwarf Thistle, Plate 44 Yellow-wort. This plate shows Common Rockrose (*Helianthemum nummularium*) and Pyramidal Orchid (*Anacamptis pyramidalis*). Secondly, there are other plants, also calcicoles, which are especially abundant on limestone but are sometimes found on other soils. Meadow and Creeping Buttercup are shown in Plates 50 and 52. This plate shows Salad Burnet *(Poterium sanguisorba*) and Lady's Bedstraw (*Galium verum*). Thirdly, there are plants which show no preference for limestone, but are likely to be there as much as anywhere else. Plates 6 and 44 show Black Medick, Plate 44 Birdsfoot Trefoil, Ragwort and Cow Parsley and Plate 52 Germander Speedwell, Restharrow and Field Scabious. This plate shows Red Clover (*Trifolium* pratense). Fungi also grow in meadows, such as Giant Puffball (Plate 73), Morel (Plate 76), waxcaps (*Hygrocybe* species), *Bolbitius vitellinus* (Plate 77) and Shaggy Inkcap (Plate 81), and mosses and lichens nestle among the grasses.

Upright Brome - dominant in some limestone meadows

Wood Cranesbill - in a Scottish meadow plant

Calcicoles l to r - Common Rockrose, Pyramidal Orchid, Salad Burnet

Lady's Bedstraw - calcicole

Red Clover - tolerant of different soils

PLATE 89. SUCCESSION AND ECOLOGY IN ACID GRASSLAND, HEATHS, MOORS AND PEAT BOGS

Acid grassland develops where the underlying rock or soil is acidic. Decay of dead plants is hindered by acidity, so a layer of humus often accumulates and hinders drainage and aeration. Over years, the humus turns into peat. Such areas are called heaths in the south and moors in the north. The surface layers can be very wet and waterlogged when it rains but very dry otherwise. Such conditions lead to a very restricted flora.. Plants may adapt by reducing water loss by having thick needle-shaped leaves with edges folded in, like Bell Heather (*Erica cinerea*), or thorns replacing leaves, such as Western Gorse (*Ulex gallii*). Since the plant material does not quickly beak down to produce mineral salts, some plants have other ways of obtaining nutrients, such as associations between their roots and fungi which break down organic materials to release nutrients, as in Heath Spotted Orchid (*Dactylorhiza ericetorum*), saprophytism, parasitism and even carnivorous habits, as in sundews and butterworts (all Plate 26).

The flora is particularly is particularly restricted on dry heaths, where the most conspicuous plants are the heaths, particularly Ling (*Calluna vulgaris*). Other typical plants are Wavy Hair Grass (*Deschampsia flexuosa*), Bilberry (*Vaccinium myrtillus*), Bearberry (*Arctostaphylos uva-ursi*), Cowberry (*Vaccinium vitis-idaea*), Gorse (*Ulex* species), Tormentil (*Potentilla erecta*), Heath Bedstraw (*Galium saxatile*) and Heath Rush (*Juncus squarrosus*). Bracken (Plate 56) often invades. Mosses, such as *Polytrichum* species (Plate 60) are common and a variety of lichens. On wetter heaths and the often even wetter northern moors, there is much Purple Moor Grass (*Molinia caerulea*) and a greater variety of other plants, including Heath Spotted Orchid, Bog Asphodel (*Narthecium ossifragum*), Lousewort (*Pedicularis sylvatica*), butterworts and sundews. In extremely wet conditions, heaths and moors can be replaced by bogs. Often, there then is a growth of Bog Moss (*Sphagnum* species) which forms a saturated mat of dead plant material devoid of soil, in which very few other plants grow. These include cottongrasses (*Eriophorum* species), various rushes and sedges, sundews and butterworts.

Communities change with time. If we think of a community as starting with bare soil and gradually changing to reach a final form, the series of stages is called a succession. This can sometimes be seen clearly on heaths and moors, since all above ground vegetation can be destroyed by fire, sometimes deliberately to maintain grouse moors in the best state for the sport, and has to start again. On a dry heath, it will often begin with grasses and agricultural weeds. Dominant heathland grasses will gradually take over, such as Wavy Hair Grass and Mat Grass (*Nardus stricta*), and there is eventually a covering of grass, heather and other heathland plants. Without regular grazing, burning or cutting of bracken or gorse, scrub invades. Gorse grows up in the shelter of heather and then, when it reaches its mature spiny state, it shelters trees in turn - firstly Birch (*Betula pendula*), then larger trees like Scots Pine and Sessile Oak (*Quercus petraea*).

Heath Spotted Orchid - on heathland

flowers

Bell Heather - needle-shaped leaves

Heath Rush - on heathland

Tormentil - heathland

Heath Bedstraw - heathland

Purple Moor Grass - moorland

Bog Asphodel

Lousewort

Peat bog with Cottongrass

Heathland succession from grassland to Gorse scrub to Birch woodland

Gorse growing up in Ling

PLATE 90: ECOLOGY OF WOODLAND AND HEDGEROWS

The structure of woods - from canopy at the top through understorey and shrub layer to ground flora - and the ways in which plants cope in woods and the similar hedgerows were described in Plate 45. Plants included were Ash, Field Maple, Spurge Laurel, Wood Anemone, Hawthorn, Traveller's Joy, Toothwort and Yellow Archangel. Scots Pine and Yew are covered in Plates 54 and 55, ferns in Plates 56-59, and mosses and liverworts in Plates 60-64.

The constituents depend partly on the underlying soil. Some trees, such as Ash and Field Maple, prefer limestone, others acid conditions, such as Birch (*Betula pendula*) and Sessile Oak (*Quercus petraea*). Common Oak (Plate 17), Hawthorn and Beech are equally at home on either. The shrubs Traveller's Joy (Plate 50), Wild privet (*Ligustrum vulgare*) and Dogwood (*Cornus sanguinea*) are very rarely found off limestone and Early Purple Orchid (Plate 15) prefers it. Foxglove (*Digitalis purpurea*), Common Cow-wheat (*Melampyrum pratense*) and Wood Sage (*Teucrium scorodonia*) prefer acid soil.

Each structural layer depends partly on what the layer above allows. Under Birch (*Betula pendula*), invaders from adjacent acid grassland occur because so much light penetrates. Common Oak (*Quercus robur*) and Ash, still provide enough light for an appreciable flora below. In the understorey are Hazel, Field Maple, Holly (*Ilex aquifolium*), Elder (*Sambucus nigra*), Hawthorn, Yew and Spindle (Plate 40). The shrub layer has Wayfaring Tree (Plate 40), Spurge Laurel, Bramble (*Rubus* species), Honeysuckle (Plate 34), Guelder-rose (Plate 16), Wild Privet, Traveller's Joy, Black Bryony (Plates 12 and 13) and Dogwood. In the herb layer an early spring patchwork might include Wood Anemone (Plate 45), Bluebell (Plates 15 and 51), Wood Avens (Plates 15 and 43), Pignut (*Conopodium majus*) and Wood Sanicle within a single square yard. Alternatively, a single species, such as Dog's mercury (*Mercurialis perennis*), can cover the ground to make use of early sunlight. Others are too numerous to list, but examples are shown in earlier plates - ferns in Plates 56 and 58, Enchanter's Nightshade (Plate 10), Early Purple Orchid, Primrose (Plate 32), Wood Anemone, Herb Paris (Plate 4), Sweet Violet (Plates 30 and 42), Moschatel (Plate 11), Ground Ivy (Plate 9) and Cuckoo Pint (Plate 35). Under Beech there is often little except fungi because of the deep shade. Fungi and non-photosynthetic plants such as Toothwort (Plate 45) and Birdsnest Orchid (Plate 26) can grow under any light conditions. There are also plants in clearings and at the edges, such as Hairy St John's Wort (Plate 9) and Red Campion (Plate 31).

The composition of a wood is variable. Ash and Oak may be dominant over much of it, while Beech may take over certain areas. Large areas often have a Hazel understory, usually planted originally and then coppiced. Herbaceous plants like Dog's Mercury and Ramsons (*Allium ursinum*) may be dominant locally. Over time, there is a succession from bare soil, which is colonized by herbaceous plants, followed by scrub, then trees. Trees casting dense shade like Beech eventually form a climax stage after a predominance of Ash and then Oak. Most woods were planted, but this sequence occurs after felling.

Oak wood **Birch wood** **Ash wood**

Beech wood **Wild privet - prefers alkaline** **Common Cow-wheat - prefers acid**

Wood Sage - preferring acid **Hazel - coppice** **Dog's Mercury - dominant**

Dog's Mercury - plant **Ramsons - dominant** **plant**

PLATE 91: ECOLOGY IN ARABLE FIELD BORDERS AND GARDENS

Plate 43 describes how plants adapt to the changing conditions of arable and garden border environments, including Ivy-leaved Speedwell, Hairy Bittercress, Wood Avens/Herb Bennett, Greater Bindweed, Ground Elder and Charlock.

The wild plant communities which develop follow the annual cycle of management. By April each year, an army of annual weeds appears, some of which began their lives by germinating in late autumn or winter, giving them a good start in the New Year. The parade includes Ivy-leaved Speedwell, Large Field Speedwell (*Veronica persica*), Grey Speedwell (*Veronica polita*) Red Deadnettle (*Lamium purpureum*), Hairy Bittercress, Shepherd's Purse (*Capsella bursa-pastoris*) and Groundsel (*Senecio vulgaris*). Other weeds appear later, like Smooth Sowthistle (*Sonchus oleraceus*) and Wood Avens, which hide among cultivated plants. Black Bindweed (*Fallopia convolvulus*), Field Bindweed (*Convolvulus arvensis*), Cleavers (*Galium aparine*) (Plate 4), Meadow Pea (*Lathyrus pratensis*) and Common Vetch (*Vicia sativa*) (Plate 8) rely on other plants for support so that only a weak stem is needed and growth can therefore be quick and seeds produced before weeding intervenes. Plants which grow and seed rapidly despite sturdy stem development include Fool's Parsley (Plate 48), Fumitory (Plates 14 and 51), Corn and Long-headed Poppy (*Papaver rhoeas* and *dubium*) (Plate 52 and 53), Scarlet Pimpernel (Plate 52), *Annual* Mercury (*Mercurialis annua*), Sun Spurge (*Euphorbia helioscopia*), Petty Spurge (Plate 4) and Black Nightshade (*Solanum nigrum*). Ground Elder (*Aegopodium podagraria*), Creeping Buttercup (*Ranunculus repens*), the bindweeds and Stinging Nettle (*Urtica dioica*) have rhizomes underground or runners close to the surface which are only partially removed by gardeners. Some plants are unusual or pretty or interesting to look at, so that gardeners may be seduced into leaving them till they have produced seeds - such as Round-leaved Fluellen (*Kickxia spuria*), Mullein (*Verbascum thapsus*), Cow Parsley (*Anthriscus sylvestris*), Common St John's Wort (*Hypericum perforatum*), Dwarf Spurge (*Euphorbia exigua*), Teasel (*Dipsacus fullonum*), Musk Mallow (*Malva moschata*) and Sleeping Beauty (*Oxalis corniculata*).

Though arable fields and gardens have many features in common, there are differences in the communities, perhaps because the management of arable fields is often of a more sweeping nature. Scentless Mayweed (*Tripleur-ospermum maritimum*) and Scented Mayweed (*Matricaria chamomila*) for instance, are arable weeds not seen much in gardens, while Petty Spurge and Wood Avens are associated more with gardens. Corn Poppy (*Papaver rhoeas*) occurs in both but in huger swathes on arable land.

The plants encountered in gardens and arable fields vary between and within communities, but there is little opportunity for a succession to develop unless there is serious horticultural neglect, and then this type of environment disappears anyway.

Ivy-leaved Speedwell, Large Field Speedwell, Grey Speedwell - clockwise from top left

Field Bindweed - garden border

Round-leaved Fluellen - on rockery

Cow Parsley - in garden border

part of plant

Sun Spurge - in garden border

Common St John's Wort - in garden border

flowers

Annual Mercury - in garden border

Scentless Mayweed -

Scented Mayweed - colony in field

Corn Poppy - colony in field

PLATE 92: ECOLOGY OF WET PLACES

The ways in which plants adapt to wet situations has been described in Plate 47, including Stream Water Crowfoot, White Waterlily, Marsh Marigold and Great Hairy Willowherb. Wet habitats include ponds, rivers, canals, streams, bogs, marshes and ditches. There are different communities in habitats with open water and those that are basically wet soil. In those with open water there are further differences between the banks and the open water itself.

In open water, the plants are either submerged or floating. Some have pollination above water, such as River-crowfoot, while in others it is underwater, such as some Water Starworts (*Callitriche* species) and Rigid Hornwort (*Ceratophyllum demersum*). Submerged non-vascular plants include Blanketweed (Plate 65), Stoneworts (Plate 68) and Willow Moss (Plates 60-61). Plants with floating leaves include Common Water Crowfoot (Plate 50), White and Yellow Waterlily (Plate 38) and Frogbit (*Hydrocharis morsus-ranae*), which root at the bottom, and duckweeds (Plate 1), which are entirely floating with roots dangling in the water. Some have both floating and submerged leaves, such as Arrowhead (*Sagittaria sagittifolia*), which also has aerial leaves.

Margins of open water have plants with some vegetative parts above the surface, known as emergent plants. Some are low-growing and able to change between submerged and emergent in response to water level changes, such as New Zealand Pigmyweed (*Crassula helmsii*). Other species have flowers well above water and aerial leaves. Some have long narrow leaves to avoid water movement damage, such as Yellow Flag (Plate 33) and Reed Canary Grass (Plate 29).

Wet soil plants commonly grow by the edge of open water, such as Alder (*Alnus glutinosa*), Hemlock Water Dropwort (*Oenanthe crocata*), Great Hairy Willow-herb (*Epilobium hirsutum*), Great Water Dock (*Rumex hydrolapathum*), and Celery-leaved Buttercup (*Ranunculus sceleratus*), and can also be emergent. Plants which grow in bogs, marshes, ditches and other wet places include Lady's Smock (Plate 52), Goat Willow (Plate 15), Marsh Arrowgrass (Plate 10), Hoary Willowherb (Plate 36), Sneezewort (Plate 52), Ragged Robin (*Lychnis flos-cuculi*) and Purple Loosestrife (*Lythrum salicaria*). Some plants grow close to water without needing wet soil, such as Black Mustard (*Brassica nigra*), Hemp Agrimony (*Eupatorum cannabinum*) and even fully terrestrial plants.

Aquatic communities vary. A riverside can be dominated by Branched Bur-reed (*Sparganium erectum*) at one point and by Indian Balsam (*Impatiens glandulifera*) at another. Dominant plants influence what other plants occur. Branched Bur-reed, for instance, forms dense stands, excluding other plants. Various types of succession also occur, and eroded areas of river bank give opportunities to observe one of them. On bare mud, delicate plants like Celery-leaved Buttercup and Water Pepper (*Petrsicaria hydropiper*) can be found. If not further disturbed, the area is gradually taken over by more vigorous plants.

Rigid Hornwort - totally submerged

Frogbit - floating leaves in pond

New Zealand Pigmyweed - submerged to emergent

Arrowhead - aerial leaves -

submerged and floating leaves

Celery-leaved Buttercup - wet soil beside river

Marsh with Marsh Marigold and willows

Ragged Robin - colony in marshy ground

plant

Purple Loosestrife - in pond

Branched Bur-reed - stand in pond

Indian Balsam - colony in river

PLATE 93: ECOLOGY OF WALLS AND ROCKS

Plate 46 dealt with the adaptations made by plants to rock surfaces, including walls. Many ferns (Plate 58 and 59), mosses (Plates 60-62) and lichens (Plates 84-86) are particularly well adapted to the dry exposed conditions found there, and are often abundant. Other plants are commonly low-growing or mat-forming - Plate 46 shows Moss Campion, Biting Stonecrop, English Stonecrop and Ivy-leaved Toadflax. It also shows Kidney Vetch with its dense woolly hairs which protect it when it grows on rocks.

On mountain rocks, plants have to survive low temperatures, snow and ice, strong winds, unstable soil, desiccation in some localities, and very short growing seasons. They are constantly threatened by grazing animals so are often found on inaccessible ledges. The plants found sometimes depend on whether the rocks are acid or alkaline. Holly Fern (*Polystichum lonchitis*) and Alpine Mouse-ear Chickweed (*Cerastium alpinum*), for instance, are normally found on alkaline rocks, while Parsley Fern (*Cryptogamma crispa*) is found on acid rocks and Starry Saxifrage (*Saxifraga stellaris*) prefers acid conditions, though it can occur elsewhere. Most of the more common mountain plants, however, can grow on either - such as Mountain Sorrel (*Oxyria digyna*), and Alpine Lady's Mantle (*Alchemilla alpina*). Yellow Mountain Saxifrage (*Saxifraga aizoides*) occurs on wet rocks.

Lowland rocks and walls are occupied by different plants, which are not adapted to mountain conditions but do have to endure drought and a low-nutrient environment. They tend to have fleshy leaves, such as English Stonecrop, Biting Stonecrop, White Stonecrop (*Sedum album*), Shining Cranesbill (*Geranium* lucidum) and Rue-leaved Saxifrage (*Saxifraga tridactylites*).

Limestone pavement is an interesting habitat found both on mountains and at sea level. It is a plateau dissected by long slits called grykes separating the remaining areas of surface stone called clints. Limestone plants such as Bloody Cranesbill (*Geranium sanguineum*) and Lady's Bedstraw (*Galium verum*) inhabit the surface, while the grykes shelter delicate plants such as Maidenhair Fern (*Adiantum capillis-veneris*).

The flora of walls partly reflects the natural rocks of the locality, though a variety of non-native plants invade mortared walls in particular - such as Ivy-leaved Toadflax, Yellow Corydalis (*Pseudofumaria lutea*) and Red Valerian (*Centranthus ruber*).

Holly Fern - on alkaline rock

Alpine Mouse-ear Chickweed - on alkaline rock

Parsley Fern - on acid rock

Starry Saxifrage - on acid rock

Mountain Sorrel - (Photo by John Kerr)

Alpine Lady's Mantle

Yellow Mountain Saxifrage - wet

Yellow Corydalis - on mortared wall

Red Valerian - on mortared wall

Limestone pavement

Bloody Cranesbill and Lady's Bedstraw - limestone pavement

Maidenhair Fern - gryke

PLATE 94: ECOLOGY OF SEAWATER HABITATS

Plate 46 described some of the adaptations found in plants in marine environments, including Rock Samphire. Plants which can survive the saltiest of these are called halophytes.

Hardly any British flowering plants grow in the sea. Seaweeds, however, grow between high and low tide levels so that they are alternately in the sea and out of it and have to cope with this. Different seaweeds grow at different levels on the shore. Plates 65-67 show a variety of them and refer to some of the adaptations required, mostly concerned with not being swept away or damaged by the tides.

Saltmarshes are extensions of the sea. They are formed by fine mud, silt or sand being carried in suspension by the tide into a sheltered area where they stay put. They are regularly inundated by sea water, and only a relatively small number of plants ("true halophytes") can cope with this. As they grow, they trap more silt, so that the level is gradually raised, with tidal waters running in channels between raised hummocks. As the ground level rises, new species appear. These trap even more solids and gradually a mat of vegetation develops. The lowest level in this succession just has seaweeds. The next has glassworts (*Salicornia* species), which, like many halophytes, are succulent, or, where the mud is soft, deep and unstable, by cord grasses (*Spartina* species), which have long anchoring roots. The next zone has such plants as Sea Aster (*Aster tripolium*), Sea Manna Grass (*Puccinellia maritima*), Common Seablite (*Suaeda maritima*), scurvygrasses (*Cochlearia* species) and Sea Purslane (*Halimione portulacoides*). Sometimes there's a next zone characterised by sea lavenders (*Limonium* species) and Thrift (*Armeria maritima*). These various zones sometimes intermingle to the extent of being unrecognizable. They are succeeded by a level where the plants might consist of grasses, rushes and such plants as Sea Milkwort (*Glaux maritima*) and Slender Haresear (*Bupleurum tenuissimum*). Sometimes, however, the upper levels are swamps, first of brackish water and then of fresh water. The brackish parts have Marsh Mallow (*Althaea officinalis*), Parsley Water Dropwort (*Oenanthe lachenalii*), Sea Clubrush (*Bolboschoenus maritima*), Wild Celery (*Apium graveolens*), Sea Barley (*Hordeum marinum*), Water Crowfoot (*Ranunculus baudotii*), Marsh Sowthistle (*Sonchus palustris*), Sea Plantain (*Plantago maritima*) and Sea Wormwood (*Artemisia maritima*).

Another habitat dominated by seawater embraces the rocks and cliffs which it constantly washes or sprays. On the steepest cliffs they usually grow in crevices in the rock where they must be able to survive on small amounts of nourishment and cope with strong winds, often by long woody roots to anchor them firmly. The most constant and typical plant is Thrift (*Armeria maritima*). It can be accompanied by Sea Campion (*Silene maritima*), Rock Sea Lavender (*Limonium binervosum*), Rock Samphire, Common Scurvygrass (*Cochlearia officinalis*), Rock Sea Spurrey (*Spergularia rupicola*), Sea Spleenwort (*Asplenium marinum*) and Sea Heath (*Frankenia laevis*).

Glassworts (*Salicornia fragilis* (front) and *ramossima*) - early saltmarsh colonists

Common Cord Grass - early saltmarsh colonist

Sea Aster - saltmarsh

Saltmarsh habitats - English Scurvy-grass

Common Sea Lavender

Common Sea Lavender - upper saltmarsh

Sea Milkwort - upper saltmarsh

Marsh Mallow - brackish to fresh water

Thrift - on sea cliff

Rock Sea Spurrey - on sea cliff

Sea Heath - on sea cliff

PLATE 95: ECOLOGY OF BEACHES, DUNES, SHINGLE AND SEA CLIFF TOPS

Plate 46 described some of the adaptations found in plants in dry marine environments - Sea Sandwort, Biting Stonecrop, English Stonecrop, Kidney Vetch, Yellow-horned Poppy and Great Sea Stock. All their habitats involve some exposure to salt, either in the water or soil or as spray, but have different communities. Some plants are halophytes, but others are xerophytes, adapted to survive in dry conditions, for instance, by needle-shaped or spiny leaves to reduce loss of water and succulent structure to store it.

The dry sand at the top of beaches is very subject to disturbance by submersion and deposition of sand and shingle. So many of the plants are annuals, such as Saltwort (*Salsola kali*), Sea Rocket (*Cakile maritima*) and Sea Beet (*Beta vulgaris*), though Sea Sandwort is perennial.

Beaches are often backed by sand dunes, which are formed by plants which grow on blown sand and trap it with their roots. In Britain almost all sand-dunes are formed by Marram Grass (*Ammophila arenaria*), which produces a mass of rhizomes and roots in the whole interior of the dune which bind it together. Other plants grow almost entirely on the landward side, protected from sea winds. Plants particularly associated with sand dunes include Sea Bindweed (Plate 48), Sea Spurge (*Euphorbia paralias*), Sea Holly (*Eryngium maritimum*), Greater Sea Spurrey (*Spergularia media*) and Large Evening Primrose (*Oenothera glaziovana*). As these early colonists die, their remains enrich the soil, allowing growth of such plants as Wild Pansy (*Viola tricolor*), Restharrow (*Ononis repens*), Common Storksbill (*Erodium cicutarium*), Lady's Bedstraw (*Galium verum*) and Burnet Rose (*Rosa spinosissima*). There is a variety of mosses, lichens, and various grasses and sedges. Shrubs may also arrive or be planted, such as Sea Buckthorn (*Hippophae rhamnoides*). Eventually you get a fixed dune, with a carpet of vegetation, merging into ordinary grassland.

Valleys - known as slacks - usually form between the dunes when sand is blown away. They have very moist soil, and often open water. The water is not salty, so marsh plants are the main inhabitants. The most characteristic plant is Creeping Willow (*Salix repens*). Other water-loving plants include marsh orchids, Round-leaved Wintergreen (*Pyrola rotundifolia*), Butterwort (*Pinguicula vulgaris*), and Ragged Robin (*Lychnis flos-cuculi*).

Shingle is made up of pebbles driven up the beach by wave action, or driven, also by waves, into an offshore bank called a bar or a spit. The seaward side and top of a shingle bank is usually bare of vegetation because of winds and salt spray, but the back is more protected. Shrubby Seablite (*Suaeda fruticosa*) is more at home on shingle than anywhere else, holding on by its extensive root system. Other inhabitants include Yellow Horned Poppy, Sea Pea (*Lathyrus japonica*), Sea Campion (*Silene maritima*) and Sea Kale (*Crambe maritima*).

On the higher parts of sea cliffs, characteristic plants are Portland Spurge (*Euphorbia portlandica*), Sea Radish (*Raphanus raphanistrum* ssp *maritimus*), Spring Squill (*Scilla verna*) and Autumn Squill (*Scilla autumnalis*).

Saltwort - on beach

Beach with Sea Rocket

Dune with Marram Grass

Sea Holly

Sand dunes and dune slack

Round-leaved Wintergreen - in dune slack

Hybrid Marsh Orchid - in slack

Shingle bank with Shrubby Seablite

Sea Kale - on shingle

Sea Radish - on sea cliff

Spring Squill - on sea cliff

PLATE 96: PLANTS AND ANIMALS

Plant communities cannot be fully understood without considering the role of animals. Firstly, they eat plants. Rabbits eat plants in meadows and foxes eat rabbits. This sequence is known as a food chain, and many food chains can be long and complicated. Butterflies and moths or their caterpillars feed on plants, sometimes specific plants. The caterpillars of the Peacock butterfly feed on Stinging Nettle leaves. The Five-spot and Six-spot Burnet Moth caterpillars feed on Birdsfoot Trefoil and clovers. Adult butterflies and moths, like honey bees (Plate 32), feed on nectar produced by flowers. The Six-spot Burnet Moth adult feeds on a wealth of meadow flowers but will also go, for instance, to Sea Holly (*Eryngium maritimum*) on sand dunes. Many birds feed on fruits and seeds. Snails feed on leaves. Shieldbugs feed by sucking plant sap. Frog tadpoles feed partly on the plant-like algae in the water. Sometimes, as with shieldbugs, the colour of the animal matches that of the plant, for camouflage.

Many insect and mite larvae develop within plant galls, which are tissues formed by a plant in response to the animals and on which the animals then feed. Walnut (*Juglans regia*), for instance, sometimes has raised areas with hollows beneath fringed with glandular hairs to protect gall-mite larvae feeding on the leaf tissues. In Creeping Yellow Cress (*Rorippa sylvestris*), in contrast, closed globular pink galls take over entire flower buds. The insects feed on the bud tissues and eventually have to eat their way out. Animals can also spread fungus disease to plants, such as Dutch Elm Disease, caused by a fungus brought in by a female bark beetle, which bores into the trunk and lays eggs. When the eggs hatch the larvae tunnel out at right angles to the chamber.

Feeding is not the only animal use of plants - Burnet moths use the stems of meadow plants to mate and pupate on and can be seen emerging from the chrysalis in spring, Some dragonfly larvae climb up plant stems to take to the air as adults, while Soldier Beetles appear to use the flower heads of umbels to catch insect prey visiting for nectar and as a mating platform. Badgers collect Bluebell leaves for bedding.

Animals also benefit plants. A variety of insects visit flowers to feed on nectar and/or pollen and bring about pollination, as described in Plates 29-35. Plates 39-40 show various ways in which animals help to disperse seeds, either in the process of feeding or carrying them on their coats. Many of these are cooperative relationships, where both parties benefit - known as symbiosis.

The huge scope of interaction is illustrated by Dog’s Mercury (Plate 90), which is eaten by six species of moth caterpillars, six species of beetle and slugs and snails. Bullfinches and greenfinches eat the seeds, and six species of hoverfly take its pollen and nectar, bringing about pollination, while red ants disperse its seeds by carrying them away to their nests, where the larvae feed only on nourishing bodies attached to them, leaving the seed in the soil to germinate.

Peacock caterpillar - on Stinging Nettle

Burnet Moth - on Sea Holly

Green Shieldbug - feeding on sap

Goldfinch - a seed feeder

Bark beetle - borings

Soldier Beetles - on a water dropwort

Burnet Moths - mating and emerging from pupa

Walnut - galls of gall-mite

Creeping Yellow Cress - galls of gall-midge

PLATE 97: RECORDING - WHY AND WHERE

We can record for our own interest and pleasure, to share information with others, or to contribute to organized recording schemes. The more organized the endeavour, the more it provides data to aid nature conservation by informing management decisions of *Wildlife Trusts* and other bodies on their reserves and local government bodies and their consultants on planning applications and local development plans. The information collected by local organizations complements data collection elsewhere to provide an indication of the nation's biodiversity heritage. This helps central Government departments and agencies, who are required to take wildlife into consideration in their plans and projects and need data for evidence, arguments and response to members of the public aiming to hold them to account.

The first form of recording likely to be undertaken is of individual species. For organized recording, the whole country is divided into 112 numbered vice-counties, based on the county boundaries in the 19th Century, but since modified. Each vice-county has a *Vice-county Recorder,* appointed by the *Botanical Society of Britain and Ireland (BSBI*), who receives records and enters them in a database. They are then conveyed to bodies collecting information on a wider area. The Wiltshire records, for instance, are sent to the *Wiltshire and Swindon Biological Records Centre* (*WSBRC*), where they are entered into a database to build up a broader county picture. They also go the *BSBI* and the national *Biological Records Centre* (*BRC*) for their databases. Local and national data is also used to produce national and/or local floras and for surveys on particular topics, such as the distribution of rare plants, plants in particular habitats, such as woodland, or plants in particular groups, such as trees.

Communities are also a focus of recording activity. The plants in a particular wood or meadow may be recorded, or the *National Vegetation Classification* (*NVC*) types present. Such activities sometimes identify sites that need special protection. When site surveys are organized, a chart is often provided listing the plants to look for and places to tick them off.

Organized recording usually has procedures to get different recorders to use the same methods and language and thus avoid confused communication. It is often related in some way to the *National Grid*, which is used in all *Ordnance Survey* maps of Great Britain. The whole country is divided into 204 squares which are each 100 kilometres square. Each is identified by two letters (e.g. ST and SU for those including Wiltshire), marked on the maps in blue capitals. These squares are further divided into 10 kilometre (or 10km) squares, each labelled by two numbers from 1 to 9. The first is shown along the top or the bottom of the map and the second at the sides. Thus, the village of Winsley in Wiltshire is partly in ST76 and partly in ST86. These are, in turn, divided into kilometre squares labelled by further numbers from 1-9 following each 10km square number. The ones in Winsley are shown opposite. Local recording sometimes focuses on 1km squares or 2km squares - called tetrads, because each contains four 1km squares.

A flora is essential for accurate identification and the identification may sometimes need to be checked by the Vc recorder or other expert. Records should be accompanied by name and date. It is helpful in some surveys to detail the habitat (e.g. wood), the numbers of plants, their distribution and frequency and the relationship to other species with it, the history (e.g. known there for 20 years) and other information (such as "self-sown from birdseed").

Site recording form

Name James Brown **Date** 28/6/2013
Location and national Grid Reference Grove Wood, Tufton, SS475602

Abundance codes (3rd column): D = dominant; A = abundant; F = Frequent; O = occasional; R = rare

Agrimony	Agrimonia eupatoria	O
Anemone, Wood	Anemone nemorosa	A
Angelica, Wild	Angelica sylvestris	O
etc		

Winsley 1km squares

	77	78	79	80	81	82	
64							
63			7963	8063	8163		
62			7962	8062	8162		
61			7961	8061	8161		
60		7860	7960	8060	8160		
59							

PLATE 98: RECORDING TECHNIQUES

In most cases, an individual grid reference is required for a record - sometimes a 1km or 10km square and sometimes a more precise location Each 1km square has a further 10 divisions numbered from 0 to 9 from the south to north and from the west to east. Each has to be placed after the corresponding 1km square digits. Thus, a solitary plant might be at grid reference ST807613, as shown. To match a location to the divisions accurately, the much worn device shown caters for the three main scales in *Ordnance Survey* maps. Though it can be photocopied at trial and error magnifications around 1.6, it is better to trace it from scratch from maps. A transparent plastic version called a romer is available cheaply on line. More precise grid references, with 8 or 10 figures, require use of a satellite based *Global Positioning System* (*GPS*) device. It is helpful, also, to give the vice-county, in which the record is made, the nearest town or village and any name for the site.

Frequency recording can be a simple matter as in a *Plantlife* Cranesbill survey, in which recorders were asked to count the number of plants they happened to see in a spot and tick one of six categories - 0, 1-10, 11-50, 51-100, 100-1000, 1000+. Sometimes, however, judgments are required, as in the commonly used DAFOR scale, which asks for a species to be labeled as dominant if it constitutes more than 50% of the plant cover, abundant for 31-50 %, frequent for 11-30 %, occasional for 6-10 % and rare for 1-5 %. For many purposes, it is sufficient to judge this without measuring.

Collection of specimens for identification or verification by experts is helpful but must not put rare plants at risk. The "1 in 20 rule" is helpful - one specimen only if there are 20 plants, or a part no bigger than one twentieth of the whole plant, a patch of plants or the seeds. However, careful field notes and photographs are sometimes sufficient. One might photograph the colony (from an identified viewpoint), a small group, a complete individual plant, vegetative features and inflorescences which are not evident from the whole plant picture and a close-up of the flower and/or fruit. A 15X magnifying lens with built-in illumination can be obtained online and digital photos taken through it.

Recording communities can be much more specialized. Systematic sampling is sometimes used, often by selecting squares of uniform size (quadrats) at random and recording all the plants within each. In linear sites, such as hedgerows and riverbanks, it is better to sample by stretches of particular length.

The technical details of recording systems vary according to need. In the recording for the Witshire Flora, for instance, each 10km square was allocated to a team of recorders, who completed record cards which the records centre staff entered into a database to enable preparation of distribution maps. Each dot in the example shown indicates occurrence in the kilometer square in that position). A table (see example) can be useful for recording by individuals.

A sample grid reference shown by a circle - 807 at top or bottom, 613 at side, therefore 807613

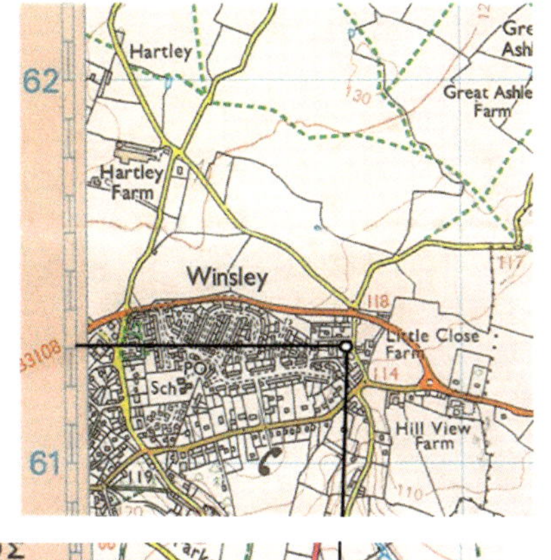

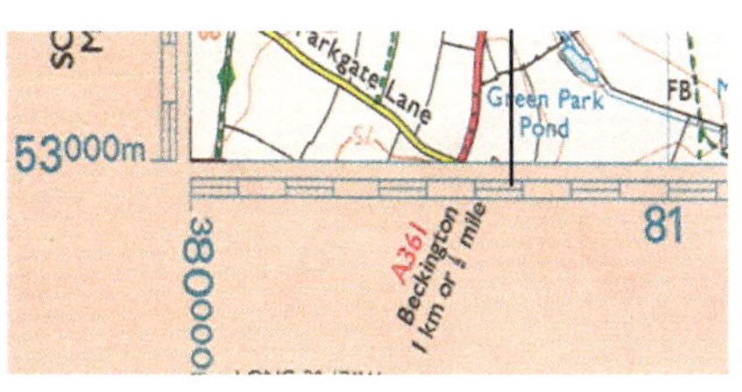

Distribution map of Bluebell (*Hyacinthoides non-scripta*) from *The Wiltshire Flora*

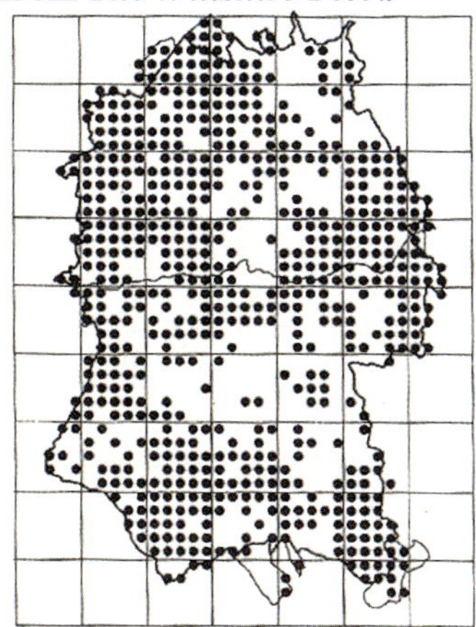

Grid reference card (about 0.6 size)

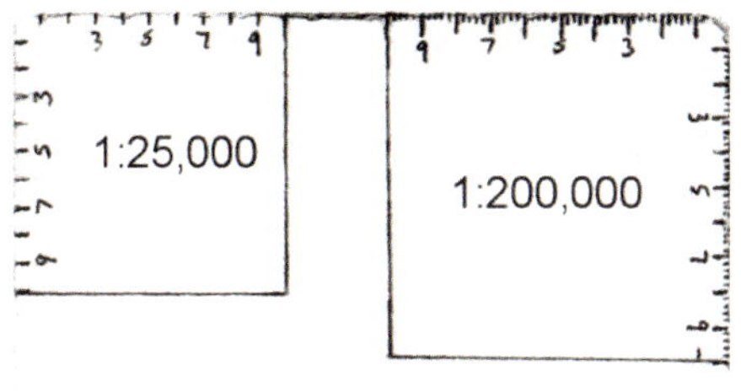

Recording table

Plant name	Date	Recorder	Site	Grid ref	Comment
Teucrium scorodonia (Wood Sage)	26/07/05	John Presland	Murhill, hedgerow	ST791609	3 plants and some more nearby
Campanula trachelium (Nettle-leaved Bellflower)	11/07/05	John Presland	Avoncliff, Becky Addy wood	ST812602	A few plants near edge of wood
Campanula trachelium (Nettle-leaved Bellflower)	26/07/05	John Presland	Conkwell, Inwoods, edge of wood	ST801634	1 plant

PLATE 99: BIODIVERSITY AND CONSERVATION

Our natural heritage has suffered assaults for centuries through cutting down of forests to make way for agriculture, industry and housing and provide timber to make dwellings, ships and so on. More recently, atmospheric pollution from factories has harmed wildlife, grassland and arable land have been sprayed with fertilizers and herbicides, rivers have been straightened and their banks made firmer to the detriment of water plants, ponds have been filled in and walls and hedges removed to increase agricultural land use, streams have been directed into pipes for safety reasons, canals have been severely dredged to improve navigation, quarries filled with refuse, grassland turned into sports fields and golf courses, etc, etc. As a result of these events, at least 150 British plant species are threatened with extinction or severe decline and vast areas of wild plant habitats have been destroyed - something like 98% of wild flower meadows, 75% of open heaths, 96% of open peat bogs and 190,000 miles of hedgerows over the past 60 years. Our countryside was once covered with dense woodland, but now only about 1.5% of the UK is taken up by ancient woodland.

In the 20th Century, resistance to these changes took the form of a nature conservation movement, which has grown and become more influential since. Current thinking is based round the concept of biodiversity. Biodiversity is a term for the variety of wildlife which we ought to be maintaining and enhancing. It refers to the existence of a large number of species of living things (e.g. Pyramidal Orchid) and variations within them, of the different communities of which they form a part (e.g. species-rich limestone grassland), and of the environments which these species and communities require (e.g. limestone grassland which has not been agriculturally improved by fertilisers, herbicides, etc). It is perhaps a definition of "nature", but with value judgments implied. In the light of this thinking, the nature conservation we embrace should maintain a wide variety of species and a variety of entire communities, rather than just rarities. Further, it should include, not just keeping what we have, but also enhancement of existing communities and creation of new ones to increase the number and variety of organisms and linking them up into networks through which species can more easily move and establish themselves more widely. Such thinking will be increasingly important as global warming causes climate, and therefore habitat, changes.

Government endorsement of this thinking started with the *United Kingdom Biodiversity Action Plan* (*UK BAP*) (1994). It described the UK's biological resources and provided a detailed plan for the protection of these resources. It initiated the compilation of a national list of Priority Species and Priority Habitats and developed action plans for most of them. The list now comprises a little over 200 species and 21 habitats, the species decisions being based on international importance, rapid decline and high risk. The criteria are very rigorous and very many rare plants are excluded, though most will be protected through belonging to priority habitats. The current coalition government published a White Paper for the Natural Environment in 2011, promising a clear institutional framework to achieve the recovery of nature. This consists of establishing *Local Nature Partnerships* (*LNPs*) to strengthen local action, creating new *Nature Improvement Areas* (*NIAs*) and operating a planning system with the protection and improvement of the natural environment as core objectives. In 2012, the work of the *United Kingdom Biodiversity Action Plan* was taken over by the *UK Post-2010 Biodiversity Framework*, which is part of an international approach organised by the *Four Countries' Biodiversity Group* and endorsed by politicians of all four UK governments.

Nature conservation involves a large number of varying bodies, so that some confusion is unavoidable. However, all Government departments have a responsibility to promote biodiversity. The *Department for Environment, Food and Rural Affairs* (*Defra*) is the one responsible for policy and regulations on it. Each Minister and Government department is supported and advised by a range of *non-departmental public bodies* (*NDPBs*), often referred to and also known as *quasi-autonomous non-governmental organisations* or *quangos,* which carry out their work at arm's length from ministers, so that they have a degree of independence. *Natural England* is the key government advisory and administrative body for biodiversity and the *Joint Nature Conservation Committee* (*JNCC*) is their major source of advice. More specific bodies include the *Inland Waterways Advisory Council* and the *National Forest Company*.

Outside Government, and theoretically independent of it, but often partially financed by it through grants, is an assemblage of organisations called *non-governmental organizations* (*NGOs*), too huge in number for major coverage here. Their main activities are campaigning, research, consultancy and ownership and/or management of nature reserves and other areas of natural importance. They include the *National Trust* and the *Royal Society of Wildlife Trusts* (*RSWT*), an umbrella body for a large number of individual *Wildlife Trusts*, covering the whole of the UK. A full list would include such specific organizations as *Vale of Glamorgan Pond Surveys* and *Birchgrove Wood Conservation* and a variety of international bodies, such as the *International Union for Conservation of Nature* (*IUCN*) and the *UN Educational, Scientific, and Cultural Organization* (*UNESCO*).

Nature conservation is subject to a variety of laws and regulations. Section 40 of the UK's *Natural Environment and Rural Communities Act* (*The NERC Act*) 2006 stating that all public authorities and their statutory undertakers must make efforts to conserve biodiversity in all of their activities and therefore have a plan for doing so. The *UK BAP Plan* is a comprehensive guide to such enterprises, providing a model on which local plans are being based. Each major Local Authority plan attempts to describe the biodiversity resources within its area, audit the activities currently promoting biodiversity, and set out targets for key habitats and species and methods of monitoring progress towards them. Local botanists could become involved in any of these activities.

PLATE 100: NATIONALLY PROTECTED AREAS

Many areas are given protection by law or under government institutions. *Sites of Special Scientific Interest* (*SSSIs*) are protected nationally, because they are the country's very best wildlife sites. The best of all are also designated as *National Nature Reserves* (*NNRs*). Many also have international status as *Special Areas of Conservation* (*SACs*). *Special Protection Areas* (*SPAs*) are primarily for birds and *Ramsars* (set up at a convention in Ramsar, Iran) for wetlands. Almost all sites will include *Priority Habitats,* many will have *Priority Species* and probably all will have rare plants and plants characteristic of the habitats present. Many other areas are protected nationally within *National Parks* and *Areas of Outstanding Natural Beauty* (*AONBs*).

The Scottish mountain Ben Lawers is an example of an *NNR* which is also an *SAC.* It has a low-nutrient loch, with Quillwort (Plate 56), and high-altitude arctic, sub-arctic and alpine communities including *Priority Species* such as Cyphel (*Minuartia sedoides*) and Mountain Sandwort (*Minuartia rubella*) and also Alpine Forget-me-not (*Myosotis alpestris*), Alpine Gentian (*Gentiana nivalis*), Alpine Lady' Mantle (Plate 93), Moss Campion (Plate 46) and Rock Speedwell (*Veronica fruticans*). Uncommon plants of wet calcareous mountain ledges are also present, with the *Priority Species* Drooping Saxifrage (*Saxifraga cernua*) and others such as Roseroot (*Sedum rosea*), Globeflower (*Trollius europaeus*), Alpine Cinquefoil (*Potentilla crantzii*) and the fern Alpine Woodsia (*Woodsia alpina*). Plants particularly likely to be seen are Yellow Mountain Saxifrage, Starry Saxifrage and Mountain Sorrel, all in Plate 93.

The Avon Gorge at Bristol is an *SSSI* likely to become an *SAC*. The steep walls support 24 rare plant species, including *Priority Species* such as two unique Whitebeams (*Sorbus* species), Fly Orchid (*Ophrys insectifera*), Bristol Rockcress (*Arabis scabra*), Spiked Speedwell (*Veronica spicata*), Honewort (*Trinia glauca*), Hutchinsia (*Hornungia petraea*), Spring Cinquefoil (*Potentilla tabernaemontani*) and Little Robin (*Geranium purpureum*).

The Lleyn Peninsula in Wales includes an *SAC* in which good quality coastal heath is protected. Mynydd Mawr shown here is part of it. It also has two rare soil lichen species. Hoselaw Loch and Din Moss in southern Scotland is an *SPA,* and therefore protected because of its birds, but also a *Ramsar*. It has the rare Cowbane (*Cicuta virosa*) in the lakeside vegetation and one of the largest and most intact areas of raised bog in the Scottish Borders. Also a *Ramsar* is Lough Corrib, the second largest lake in Ireland, which supports one of the largest areas of wetland vegetation in the country.

Wild Purbeck is one of the new *Nature Improvement Areas* (*NIAs*), which includes *SSSIs*, *NNRs* and *SACs* within an area from Poole Harbour and westwards in Dorset. It has internationally important heathlands, the harbour itself, dunes, sea cliffs, valley wetlands and much more.

Ben Lawers

Cyphel - Ben Lawers

Roseroot - Ben Lawers

Avon Gorge

Spiked Speedwell - Avon Gorge

Bristol Rockcress - Avon Gorge

Honewort - Avon Gorge

Coastal heath with Bluebells at Mynydd Mawr

Hoselaw Loch with Cowbane

Marsh Pennywort (*Hydrocotyle vulgaris*) - in Lough Corrib

Dorset Heath (*Erica ciliaris*) - on Purbeck heathland

Early Spider Orchid *Ophrys sphegodes*) - on Purbeck sea cliff

PLATE 101: LOCALLY PROTECTED AREAS

Many areas of land not nationally protected are managed to maintain and improve their biodiversity. *Wildlife Trusts* have nature reserves, some run in cooperation with owners. *Local Wildlife Sites* (*LWSs*) are monitored by a partnership of a *Wildlife Trust*, a *Local Authority*, *Natural England* and other bodies, but are mostly privately owned and managed. Protected roadside verges are mostly managed by *Wildlife Trusts* and *Local Authorities* in partnership. The *Environment Agency* oversees rivers, lakes and some ponds. Voluntary organisations such as the *RSPB* and the *Woodland Trust* own land. Here, Wiltshire is taken as an example of local protection.

Green Lane Wood is a *Wiltshire Wildlife Trust* nature reserve with Greater Butterfly Orchid (*Platanthera chlorantha*) and Violet Helleborine (*Epipactis purpurata*) from the *Wiltshire Rare Plants Register* and other woodland plants, including Early Purple Orchid (Plate 15), Bugle (*Ajuga reptans*) and Solomon's seal (*Polygonatum multiflorum*). There is also a variety of fungi.

A small, steep limestone meadow in West Wiltshire provides a helpful example of a *Local Wildlife Site*. There are 17 indicators of calcareous grassland recorded, and six other grassland indicators. There are particularly fine displays of Lesser Knapweed (*Centaurea nigra*) and Field Scabious (*Knautia arvensis*). Primrose (*Primula vulgaris*) (Plate 32) and Cowslip (*Primula veris*) (Plate 36) grow close to each other and hybridise to form the False Oxlip. Yellow-wort (Plate 44) has been recorded. The site has been grazed lightly and periodically by sheep. Two nearby LWSs have been further protected as Parish Council nature reserves and are maintained by volunteers.

A South Wiltshire protected roadside verge has a combination of grassland, wetland and woodland flora. Hard Fern (Plate 59) and Tormentil (*Potentilla erecta*) are inhabitants unusual in Wiltshire as acid soil plants. The uncommon hawkweed *Hieracium vulgatum* is present.

The River Avon is owned and managed by the *Environment Agency*. It hosts many plants typical of a riverside habitat, including three species from the *Wiltshire Rare Plants Register* - Greater Dodder (Plate 26), River Water Crowfoot (Plate 50) and Loddon Pondweed (*Potamogeton nodosus*). A recent survey found 17 wetland indicators, including Water Plantain (Plate 10), Yellow Waterlily (Plate 38), White Waterlily (Plate 47), Arrowhead (Plate 92), and Branched Bur-reed (Plate 92).

A voluntary body, the *Woodland Trust*, owns and manages Clanger and Picket Woods, near Trowbridge, also an *SSSI*. It has broad-leaved woodland with Pedunculate Oak, Ash and Hornbeam and many woodland herbs, including Moschatel (Plate 11) and Early Purple Orchid. Over forty plant species indicative of ancient woodland have been recorded.

Bugle - Green Lane Wood

Greater Butterfly Orchid - Green Lane Wood

Violet Helleborine - Green Lane Wood

LWS meadow - Lesser Knapweed

Field Scabious -

LWS meadow - Primrose

Cowslip

False Oxlip

Solomon's Seal - Green Lane Wood

Protected verge in South Wiltshire - view

Hawkweed

PLATE 102: NATURE CONSERVATION ACTIVITIES

Among many potential nature conservation activities on sites generally, a conservation worker might record plants and animals, erect fences to control access of humans or animals, construct paths or steps to improve access, control invasive plants, plant or seed areas in need of improvement, or design or erect notices and display boards. Making other people aware of biodiversity and the need to behave in ways to promote it is of major importance. Some workers may also be involved in management decisions, such as setting up grazing regimes, planned replanting, restoring bends and shallow areas in straightened and channeled rivers, building shelves in canals for marginal plants, designing safety procedures and establishing agricultural practices which encourage wildlife.

On grassland areas, conservation workers might remove invading trees or scrub or clear cut vegetation from the site to reduce fertility and discourage over-vigorous plants.

In woodland, they might remove trees and shrubs which were too crowded for healthy growth or shading out ground flora, coppice hazel, remove invasive plants which threaten native species - like Spanish Bluebell (*Hyacinthoides hispanica*), which hybridizes with English bluebells (Plate 51), or watch out for diseases which kill native trees, like Ash Dieback and Dutch Elm Disease.

On wetlands, they might remove plants or silt which threaten the continued existence of a pond, pull or dig out invasive plants, create or restore ponds or plant willows or plants like Common Reed where banks have to be stabilized.

On arable land, they might watch out for overuse of fertilizers and herbicides, make or repair border hedges or dry stone walls, or remove plants like Ivy, brambles and Traveller's Joy to prevent them from covering the wall surfaces and killing off other wall dwellers.

In gardens, they could allow early weeds to grow and set seed before serious weeding (Plate 43), have a wild flower patch, introduce a few wild plants from local seed, give a home to a rarity, avoid using weed or moss killers, control over-dominant plants (such as dandelions and daisies) to allow a varied community of wild plants and tolerate wild invaders which are not too incompatible with other gardening objectives.

On maritime sites, they might participate in building or maintaining barriers to prevent sand or shingle being swept away or plant grasses and shrubs to stabilize dunes.

In moorland areas, they could help in programmes of burning heather to allow regeneration and give opportunities for a wider range of plants to grow alongside it or cut down shrubs and trees colonising to excess.

Erecting sheep fencing

Rebuilding dry stone wall

Clearing scrub in meadow

Pond almost lost

Removing excess vegetation

Pond restored and advertised

Nature reserve signpost

Weasel's Snout (*Misopates orontium*) seeded in border

Rock Cinquefoil (*Potentilla rupestris*) - *Protected Species* grown in rockery

Sea Buckthorn (*Hippophae rhamnoides*) - stabilising dune

Patches where heather burned in Scottish Highlands

Stile and dog gate at Winsley Parish nature reserve

PLATE 103: EXPLAINING PLANT DEVELOPMENT

Previous plates have shown how plants, fungi, lichens and algae feed, grow, move and reproduce. The underlying mechanisms are complex, but an attempt is made here to describe and explain them.

Firstly, there is the question of how it is possible for an individual organism to develop and function. Normal development is determined by a combination of inherited characteristics and environmental influences. It starts off with a number of cells, more or less as shown opposite. Each cell is bounded by a cell wall made of a substance called cellulose. The bulk of the cell is occupied by one or more cavities, filled with a fluid called cell sap. The outer part is filled with a rather jelly-like material called cytoplasm. Somewhere in this is a more or less spherical body called the nucleus. There are also a large number of smaller bodies called plastids (including the chloroplasts which hold the chlorophyll) and mitochondria. From this basic structure, cells develop in varying ways to fit their different functions in different parts of the mature plant.

The nucleus contains thread-like bodies called chromosomes, which consist of strings of complex chemicals referred to as genes which determine what characteristics the plant will have and what processes it will use. The chromosomes are spiral in shape and arranged in intertwined pairs. They are called homologous pairs, because each gene on a chromosome has a complementary gene in the same position on the partner chromosome which determines the same character, though often in a different way. These two versions of the gene are called alleles. If a particular pair of alleles determines flower colour, we can imagine that one might want the flower colour to be red, while the other might want it to be white. Sometimes the two alleles are as strong as each other, in which case the flower might be pink. In many cases, however, one allele overpowers the other. If the red allele is the stronger, it is called the dominant allele and the flowers will be red. The white allele is recessive and cannot express itself in the presence of the red allele. So only if both alleles want white can the flower be white.

In practice, however, things are much more complex. Dominance and recessiveness may be only partial, more than one gene may be involved in the determination of a particular character, the action of one gene can be modified by the influence of another, and so on. “Gene” and “allele” are often used interchangeably, to complicate matters further.

Plants grow by the division of their earliest cells into other cells, which then grow to full size and themselves divide. Division involves a process called mitosis, in which every chromosome divides into two identical halves (called chromatids) and the resulting two sets are incorporated into two “daughter cells”, so that each has the same chromatids (now chromosomes) and therefore the same genetic characteristics. A diagram opposite shows what happens to a single pair of chromosomes - shown short and straight rather than long and spiral as they really are. The same happens to all the others.

Eventually, however, different cells take on different structures and functions to form particular plant organs for different purposes. This is determined by chemical reactions promoted by the genes to produce and increase the living material in the cell and the transmission and action of chemical substances which can be called plant hormones, which bring about changes at their destinations. The process is also affected by a whole host of environmental factors, such as availability of water and nutrients, light intensity, day length, temperature and so on.

A basic plant cell

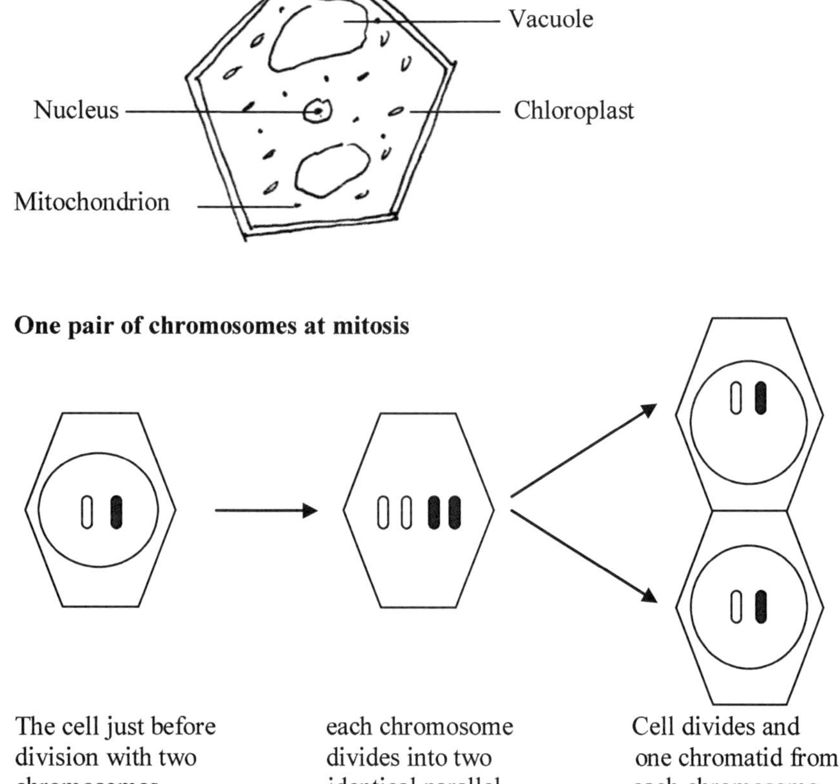

One pair of chromosomes at mitosis

The cell just before division with two chromosomes

each chromosome divides into two identical parallel halves (chromatids)

Cell divides and one chromatid from each chromosome goes to each daughter cell, both genetically identical to mother cell and to each other

PLATE 104: EXPLAINING INHERITANCE

Plants of the same species have very similar sets of genes, which goes some way towards explaining why they resemble each other, and are different from plants of a different species, which have genes showing greater differences. The genes are passed from parent to offspring, so that the latter resemble the former. At sexual reproduction, each male pollen grain and female embryo sac consists of a single cell. These cells are produced by a process of cell division called meiosis, shown in the diagram featuring just one chromosome. In meiosis, a single "mother cell" in the anther or ovule divides to form two "daughter cells", each with just one of each homologous pair of chromosomes, so that they are genetically different. Note that the chromosome divides into chromatids just as in mitosis. However, instead of individual chromatids going to different daughter cells, each pair of chromatids does this. The daughter cells are, therefore, genetically different from each other as well as from the mother cell.

There is, however, more to it than that. Before separation of the two pairs of chromatids into the two daughter cells, they twine round each other, become attached and then break apart again. In the process, parts of each chromatid can break off and then become reincorporated in a different place or a different way round, or even transfer to any of the other three chromatids. This means that parts of the parental chromosomes and their constituent genes are redistributed in a not very predictable way. This makes the two daughter cells even more different genetically from each other and from the mother cell.

Once the formation of daughter cells is complete, each divides again. This time, the two chromatids in each pair separate, one going into each of the new cells to become a chromosome in that cell. The result is four reproductive cells, all with half the number of chromosomes (known as the haploid number) of the parent (the diploid number). Since these chromosomes are, as a result of the exchange of material during the earlier stages of meiosis, different from each other, these four cells are genetically different from each other and from the original mother cell. In the stamens, they develop into four pollen grains. In the ovule, only one of them (it could be any of them) develops into an embryo sac.

At pollination, each successful pollen grain enters an ovule and fertilises its embryo sac. This consists of uniting with it to form a single cell called a zygote, which grows into the new plant. It brings together the two sets of chromosomes, so that the new individual now has the same number of chromosomes as the parent, though they are different in content and structure. The zygote then divides to start the growth of the new organism. In practice, of course, there are many pollen grains and many ovules, so that many zygotes can be formed.

The implications of the overall process of sexual reproduction are that the offspring have many genes which are the same as the two parents, and will therefore resemble them both, but, because of the recombination of genes which occurs, they will also have differences from both parents. Furthermore, the redistribution of genes means that the different offspring will also differ from each other. The redistribution has its limits, however, and the range of genes, and therefore characteristics of the plants, will mean that they are still recognisable as belonging to the same species.

One pair of chromosomes at meiosis

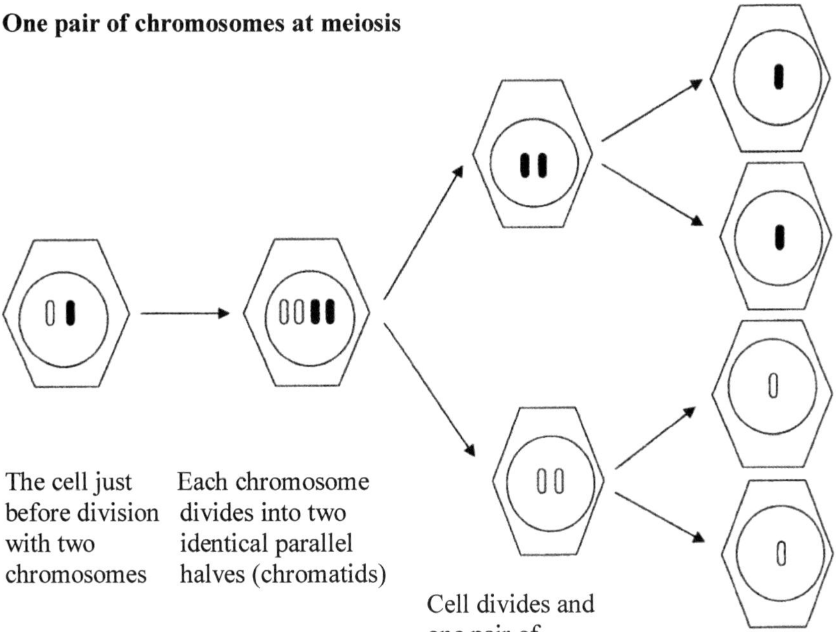

The cell just before division with two chromosomes

Each chromosome divides into two identical parallel halves (chromatids)

Cell divides and one pair of chromatids goes to each daughter cell

Each daughter cell divides again, with each chromatid going to one of four "niece" cells

Changes in chromosomes at fertilization

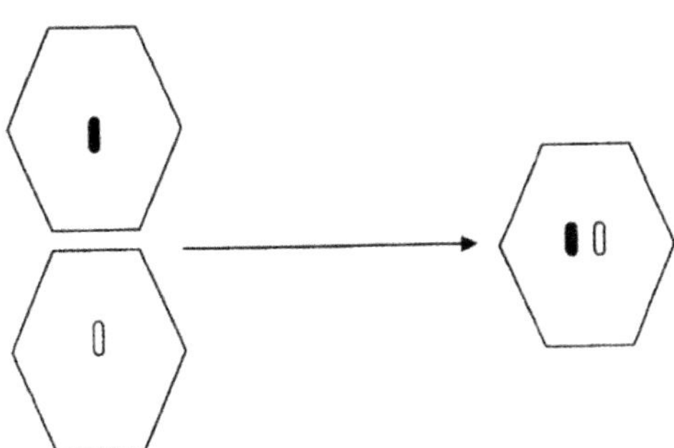

Two kinds of reproductive cells each with one chromosome

Zygote with two chromosomes

PLATE 105: GENES AND PLANT CHARACTERS

In the light of the cell division processes above, let us look again at dominance and recessiveness, illustrated by the distinction between white and yellow flowers in sweet peas. Yellow is dominant to white, so there has to be a white factor from both parents for the flowers to be white. There are three possible combinations of the two alleles involved;

- yellow allele + yellow allele - plant yellow
- yellow allele + white allele - plant yellow
- white allele + white allele - plant white.

Suppose we cross a plant with two yellow alleles with a plant with two white alleles. In the meiosis diagrams, assume that the white chromosome is the one with the white allele and the shaded one with the yellow. In the plant with the two yellow alleles, the meiotic division produces embryo sacs or pollen grains each with one yellow allele. In the same way, in the plant with two white alleles one white allele is present in each of these cells. At fertilisation, the only possible combination in a zygote is one white allele and one yellow allele, so all plants will be yellow. If we cross two of these plants, however, the process of meiosis in each parent gives embryo sacs or pollen grains each with just a single white allele or a single yellow allele. Each zygote will again have two alleles, but the nature of these alleles depends on what it has inherited from each parent. There are four alternative patterns, all equally likely to occur:

- a yellow allele from the male parent and a yellow allele from the female parent - flower yellow
- a yellow allele from the male parent and a white allele from the female parent - flower yellow
- a yellow allele from the female parent and a white allele from the male parent - flower yellow
- a white allele from the female parent and a white allele from the male parent - flower white

Since they are all equally likely, then, if there are a large number of offspring, there will, in theory, be an equal number of each combination. This means that for every white plant there will be three yellow - a phenomenon famously called the 3:1 ratio, which is typical of this kind of inheritance. Breeding experiments with sweet peas do actually produce approximately this ratio. The process is shown diagrammatically opposite. In practice, the ratios are only approximate, because not every fertilisation attempt succeeds and not every offspring survives and the precise number of individuals with each combination of alleles is a matter of chance. If, of course, a plant with a white and a yellow allele were crossed with a plant with two yellow alleles, all plants would be yellow.

These calculations apply to only this particular pattern of inheritance. If the yellow or white colour were dependent on two genes in combination, the mathematics and the experimental results would be different. Remember also that dominance and recessiveness apply only to some forms of inheritance.

This simple mechanism helps us to understand the more complex mechanisms which are commoner in the wild. For instance, Greater Knapweed is said to have five alleles known to affect flower colour in combination. In Common/Corn Poppy (*Papaver rhoeas*), including the Shirley Poppy, an even more complicated mechanism has been suggested. There is one main gene with one allele producing the full red colour, but one or more others giving a range from white to pale red or striped Yet other genes produce a dark centre, a flushed white centre, a white edge, diluted red colour and purple. Genetic mechanisms affect other characters too. In Primrose, there are two possible style lengths, as described in Plate 32, and the short style is dominant and the long style recessive, but again there may be other genes complicating the picture.

The importance of the chromosomes in inheritance has long been known. It has emerged more recently, that there can also be genetic material in the plastids and mitochondria, which can divide and reproduce independently of the rest of the plant cell they inhabit. Some inheritance from the female parent can, therefore, be brought about outside the cell nucleus.

Inheritance in sweet peas (yellow dominant, white recessive)

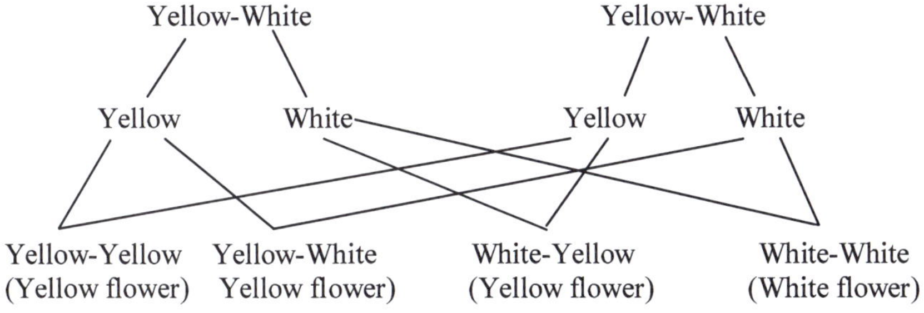

Corn Poppy - red and white flowers **white flower**

PLATE 106: EVOLUTION

Evolution is an explanation of how the range of organisms we are considering appeared on Earth. The view current among botanists in the early 19th Century was that, in describing and naming different 'kinds' of organisms, they were discovering a divine pattern in the world in which these 'kinds' were related to each other according to some creation scheme. It had been fixed by God, who had separately created all the 'kinds' at the same time. New species could not occur. Evolution replaced this with the notion that all species in existence today have descended from different species which existed in the past.

Evolutionary thinking assumes that life started over 3,500 million years ago. It began with small, simple organisms. From these evolved larger and more complicated species, which then gave rise to even more complex beings. In most cases the species from which today's species have arisen have become extinct. The sequence in which the main groups in this book appeared is shown opposite. It is assumed that the earliest living organisms lived in water with terrestrial plants evolving from them. A time of first appearance (in millions of years ago) is given for each group to give some impression of the time scale involved, but it is notional, since much is uncertain or controversial. Note that no group is shown as evolving from another group, but just as having common ancestry.

The details of evolutionary sequences are much debated. It may, however, be helpful to indicate the kinds of evolutionary change which are thought to have occurred in flowering plants, since these are the groups most studied by amateur naturalists. It seems likely that the earliest had flowers consisting of stamens and carpels, with no petals and sepals. Once the latter appeared, a list of common trends is largely accepted: woody to herbaceous; perennial to biennial to annual; deciduous to evergreen; spirally arranged leaves to opposite and whorled; spirally arranged floral parts to whorled; simple leaves to compound; net veining of leaves to parallel; many similar to fewer dissimilar floral parts; perianth of similar segments to division into petals and sepals; radially symmetrical flowers to bilaterally symmetrical; petals to absence of petals; free petals to joined; separate stamens and carpels to joined; superior ovary to inferior; solitary flowers to inflorescence; male and female flowers on the same plant to on separate plants. To illustrate this, White Waterlily (*Nuphar lutea*) (Plate 47) is regarded as an early flowering plant and has a number of features regarded as "primitive". It has numerous, spirally arranged perianth segments not divided into petals and sepals, and neither they nor the numerous stamens and carpels are joined. The Ranunculaceae, whose classification has featured in Plate 50, shows various steps forward from this, though it can't be assumed that they form an actual evolutionary sequence. Marsh Marigold (Plate 8), Old Man's Beard (*Clematis vitalba*) (Plate 50), and Wood Anemone (Plate 31) all illustrate a step forward from waterlilies in that the floral parts are in whorls rather than spirally arranged. However, the perianth is still not divided into petals and sepals, the number of stamens and carpels is large, and no floral parts are joined.

Hellebores (Plates 8 and 50) show further advances, in that there are only 2-5 carpels and they are slightly fused at the base, and the sepals and petals are different, the latter taking the form of small tubular nectaries to attract insects for pollination. Columbine also has a small number of carpels (five), and shows an additional advanced feature - a spur on each petal which contains nectar (Plate 14). The monkshoods (*Aconitum* species) are another group with a small number of carpels fused at the base, and have some additional advanced features. They also have petals taking the form of nectaries, but have another step towards complexity in that the coloured sepals are arranged in a bilaterally symmetrical manner, with the upper one forming an elongated hood (Plate 50). The buttercups (*Ranunculus* species) and Lesser Celandine (*Ficaria verna*) (Plates 11 and 28) have the same primitive features as Marsh Marigold and Wood Anemone, except that the perianth is differentiated into colourful petals and green sepals (Plates 9, 50 and 52). Pheasant's Eye (*Adonis annua*) has a clear differentiation of petals and sepals and illustrates the whorled arrangement of parts rather well. Plate 52 shows further advances in floral complexity in more advanced families.

Evolutionary sequence of main groups

PLATE 107: EVIDENCE FOR EVOLUTION

Evidence for evolution comes from many sources, and fits too well with the notion to make disbelief reasonable. Firstly, there is evidence that species can change. Plant breeders, for instance, starting from wild plants, have produced edible carrots and parsnips with thick root which are much easier on the teeth than the wild ones. The study of plant abnormalities offers further evidence. Many species with coloured flowers occasionally produce white ones. Common Centaury (*Centaurium erythraea*) normally has 5 petals but a plant has been found with10 petals and two additional similar structures - a double flower. In species of *Linaria* an abnormality known as peloria is even more striking. Peloria is the development of radially symmetrical flowers in plants whose flowers are normally bilaterally symmetrical. In Common Toadflax (*Linaria vulgaris*), this produces a form much like one of the plant's supposed ancestors. None of these examples are indisputably new species. However, Red and White Campion (*Silene dioica* and *latifolia*), always described as different species, often cross to produce hybrids with pink flowers, not clearly either species.

Secondly, various sources of evidence fit too well with the system of classification we have developed to be explicable in any reasonable way other than by the evolution of current species from earlier ones. The time sequence in which plant fossils have occurred fits with the relationships between contemporary plants - waterlilies are believed to be early in the evolutionary tree and one of the earliest flowering plant fossils is a tiny waterlily from the period lasting from 125-115 million years ago. Similarities and differences in the structure and functioning of plants are hard to interpret unless we assume a common origin for all the species. The similarities and differences within buttercups (Plate 50) also seem to require such an explanation. The ways in which plants develop similarly in different species (Plates 19-26) and the classification of flowering plants (Plate 50) also reflect a regular occurrence of many species apparently based on the same pattern of characteristics. The chemical similarities and differences in the chromosomes of different species (referred to as DNA) are further evidence. Everything points to derivation of many different species from a common pattern and according to a common system of operation.

Some sources of evidence are particularly powerful - vestigial structures, for instance, which have no function and can be thought of only as left over from an ancestor which had a use for them. An example is Common Figwort (*Scrophularia nodosa*), where flowers with four stamens are thought to have evolved from an ancestor with five, the position of the fifth occupied by a functionless staminode (Plate 12). Another is the evidence from geographical distribution. Of the 1800 flowering plants and ferns in New Zealand, three quarters are found native nowhere else (termed endemic) - the Kauri Tree (*Agathis australis*) is an example. Another seventy or so are found only in New Zealand and Australia. But gum trees (*Eucalyptus* species), wattles and bottlebrushes, abundant in East Australia, are absent as natives from New Zealand. It is as though the plants arose from separate evolutionary pathways in parts of the world originally joined to but later cut off from elsewhere.

The Galapagos Islands, off the northwest coast of South America, provide even stronger evidence. They emerged from the sea through volcanic activity. They have 749 species of vascular plant, of which 216 are found nowhere else, but resemble plants on the South American mainland. As an example, they have 14 taxa of the Prickly Pear Cactus (*Opuntia* species) which resemble mainland species but are endemic to the Galapagos Islands. They belong to six different species, each taxon occurring on only one or more particular islands, where it is likely that they have arrived from the mainland and evolved on each island in isolation.

Common Centaury - normal and double flower

Common Toadflax - normal flowers

peloric flowers

Kauri Tree - New Zealand endemic

***O. galapageia* var. *profusa* - Rabida**

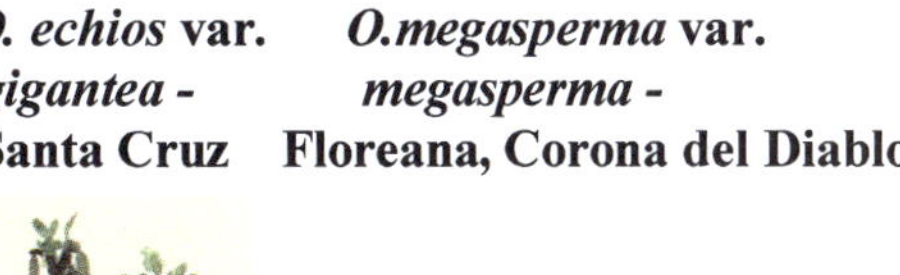

***O. echios* var. *echios* - Baltra, Santa Cruz, Daphne**

***O. echios* var. *gigantea* - Santa Cruz**

***O.megasperma* var. *megasperma* - Floreana, Corona del Diablo**

PLATE 108: MECHANISM OF EVOLUTION

The only convincing sounding theory we have to explain evolution is the theory of natural selection, put forward by Charles Darwin and Alfred Russell Wallace in the mid-19th Century. Its name is misleading, since no selection is involved. It is metaphorical. The theory can be described as follows.

- Living organisms vary.
- Some of the variations give the organisms an advantage over organisms without them in the particular environment which they inhabit.
- Since resources are limited, there is a struggle for existence and only some individuals of a species can survive.
- Those with variations which give them an advantage will, in the long-term, survive while others will die out.
- Those that survive will pass on their changed nature to their descendents so that the changes will persist.
- Over millions of years, many instances of this process will change one species into another.

Variations caused by differing environmental conditions cannot normally be passed from parent to offspring. The relevant variations are genetically determined. Some occur when the genes are redistributed during reproduction (Plate 105). Some biologists think a large number of such changes could lead to new species over many millions of years. Others think larger changes are necessary, such as those resulting from mutations and chromosome doubling.

Mutations are changes beyond the range normally found in a species. They can consist of alterations in the chemical nature of a single allele or additions, deletions or transfers of lengths of chromosomes. Environmental influences are thought to cause some of them. An example is the range of occasional abnormal forms of Foxglove (*Digitalis purpurea*) known collectively as the 'Heptandra' mutant. One of its forms has split petals, and can be seen in some garden centres under the name *Digitalis* 'Serendipity'.

Chromosome doubling is known technically as polyploidy. For example, Common Valerian (*Valeriana officinalis*) has two races in Britain. Chromosome numbers are given in floras as the diploid (2n) ones found in the vegetative cells of the plant. One grows in limestone grassland and has 28 chromosomes, while the other is in wet places and has 56. It looks as though this has resulted from a doubling of chromosomes within the same species. It can also occur when two species hybridise, which can lead to greater differences from the original.

We have observed natural selection within a species, as in Self-heal (*Prunella vulgaris*), which grows upright in meadows but prostrate in lawns to adapt to the mowing regimes. Some plants continue to grow prostrate if cultivated without mowing, so it is reasonable to assume they are genetically different. It seems highly probable that the prostrate form is sometimes brought about by a mutation, and has selective advantage. The evolution of a new species, however, could take millions of years, which would make it unobservable. It would be quicker with large mutations. Most of them are disadvantageous to the plant, but some could survive as new species, particularly if they coincided with a major change in the environment.

The processes described above may be only part of the explanation of evolutionary change. A field of study called epigenetics has shown that some characteristics acquired by a plant during its lifetime can be passed on by bodies in the reproductive cells other than chromosomes, as in the peloric condition described in Common Toadflax in Plate 107.

Natural selection is a framework of ideas which enables us to interpret the variety of living things in a logical way. It has defects as a scientific theory in that it does not allow us to predict what will happen in the future. In any case, it is flexible enough to explain anything, so it would not be possible to set up experimental tests which could invalidate or confirm such predictions, and thence the theory. A helpful way of looking at it is that species are constructed and interrelated as though they had evolved in this way.

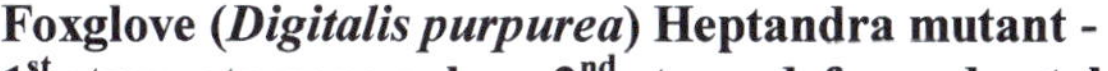

Foxglove (*Digitalis purpurea*) Heptandra mutant -

1st stage, stamens only **2nd stage, deformed petals** **'Serendipity'**

Common Valerian **Self-heal - normal form** **prostrate on a lawn**

ABOUT THE AUTHOR

John Presland studied botany at St Catharine's College, Cambridge, taught it to A and S levels for a few years and then pursued a career as an educational psychologist. Botany remained a hobby, both at home and abroad, for over 50 years. He became secretary and then chairman of the *Sutton Coldfield Natural History Society*, is now a long-term committee member of *Wiltshire Botanical Society* and has edited their scientific journal *Wiltshire Botany* for 16 years. A range of voluntary conservation activities have engaged him - *Wildlife Trust* nature reserve warden, protected road verge monitor, parish nature reserve organizer, regular recorder of plants and fungi, including recording for the *Wiltshire Flora* and the *Wiltshire Rare Plants Register*, and self-appointed promoter of the flora of dry stone walls. He has cultivated wild plants and taken many photographs. John has written about his activities regularly, and has contributed articles to *Wiltshire Botany,* the *Newsletter* of *The Botanical Society of the British Isles (BSBI)* and various other journals and periodicals. This work has extended to two booklets, one on the flora of limestone dry stone walls and one (with other authors) on abnormalities in plants, Much of the content of the website www.dry-stone-wall-flora.co.uk is his. For many years, he has given talks on botany, illustrated by colour slides, to a wide variety of groups. Throughout his working life, and during his retirement, he has read botanical publications and sought help from more experienced botanists to try to keep abreast of advances in knowledge. He is married with children and grandchildren.

Made in the USA
Charleston, SC
27 February 2014